1950s M

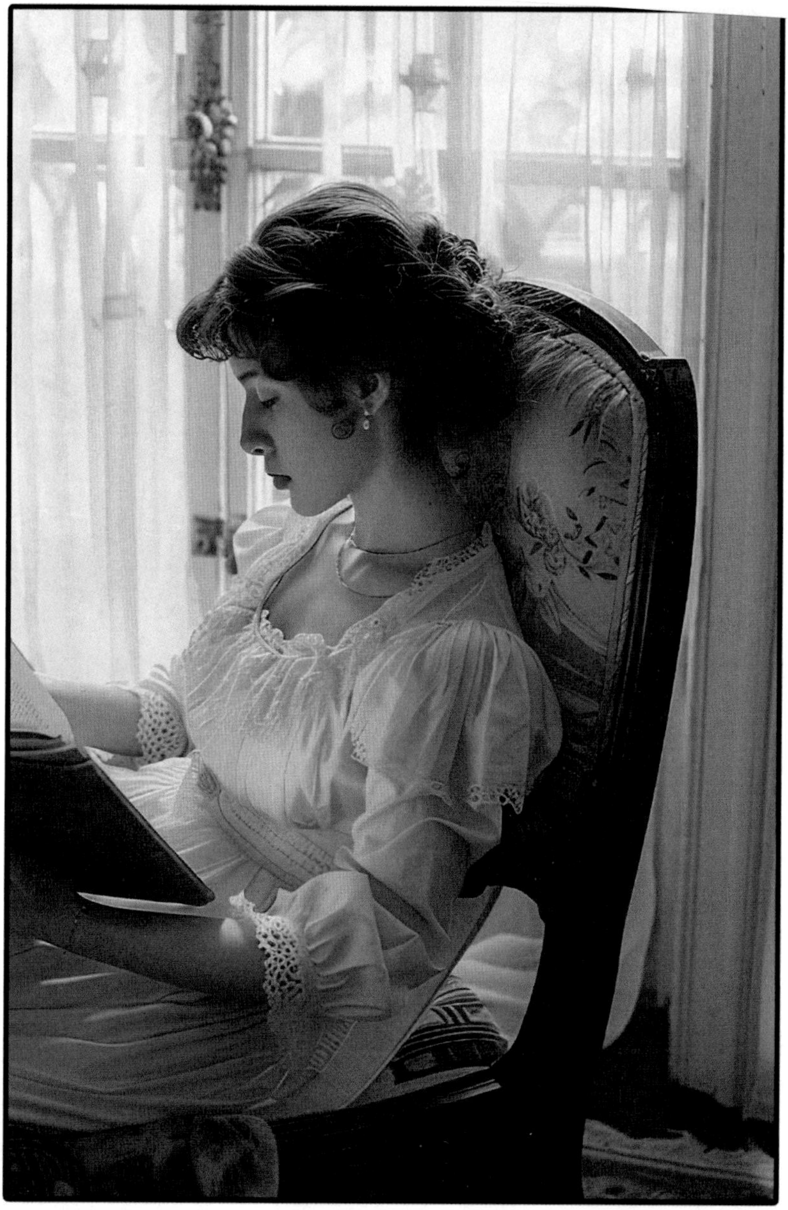

Monica Austin

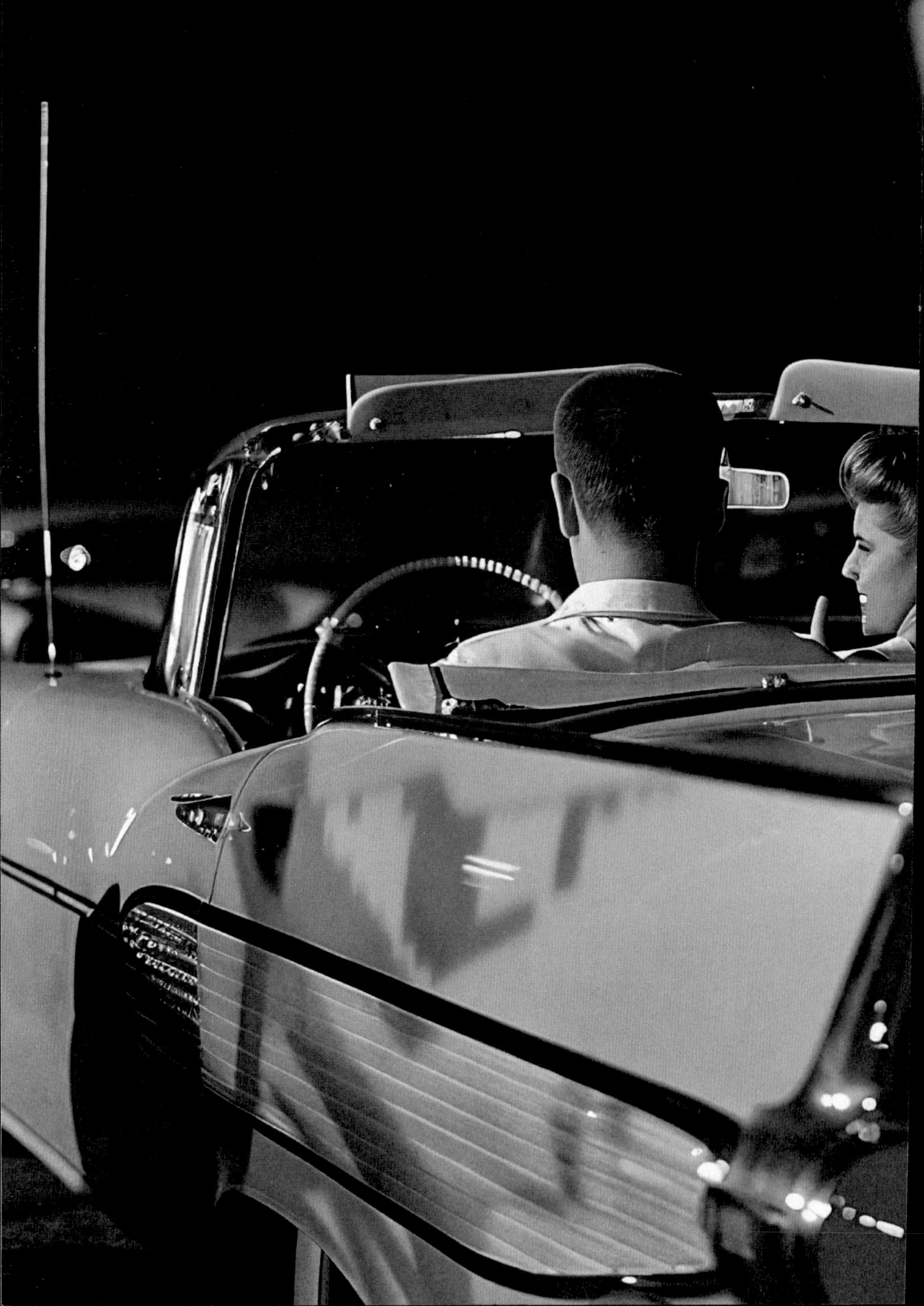

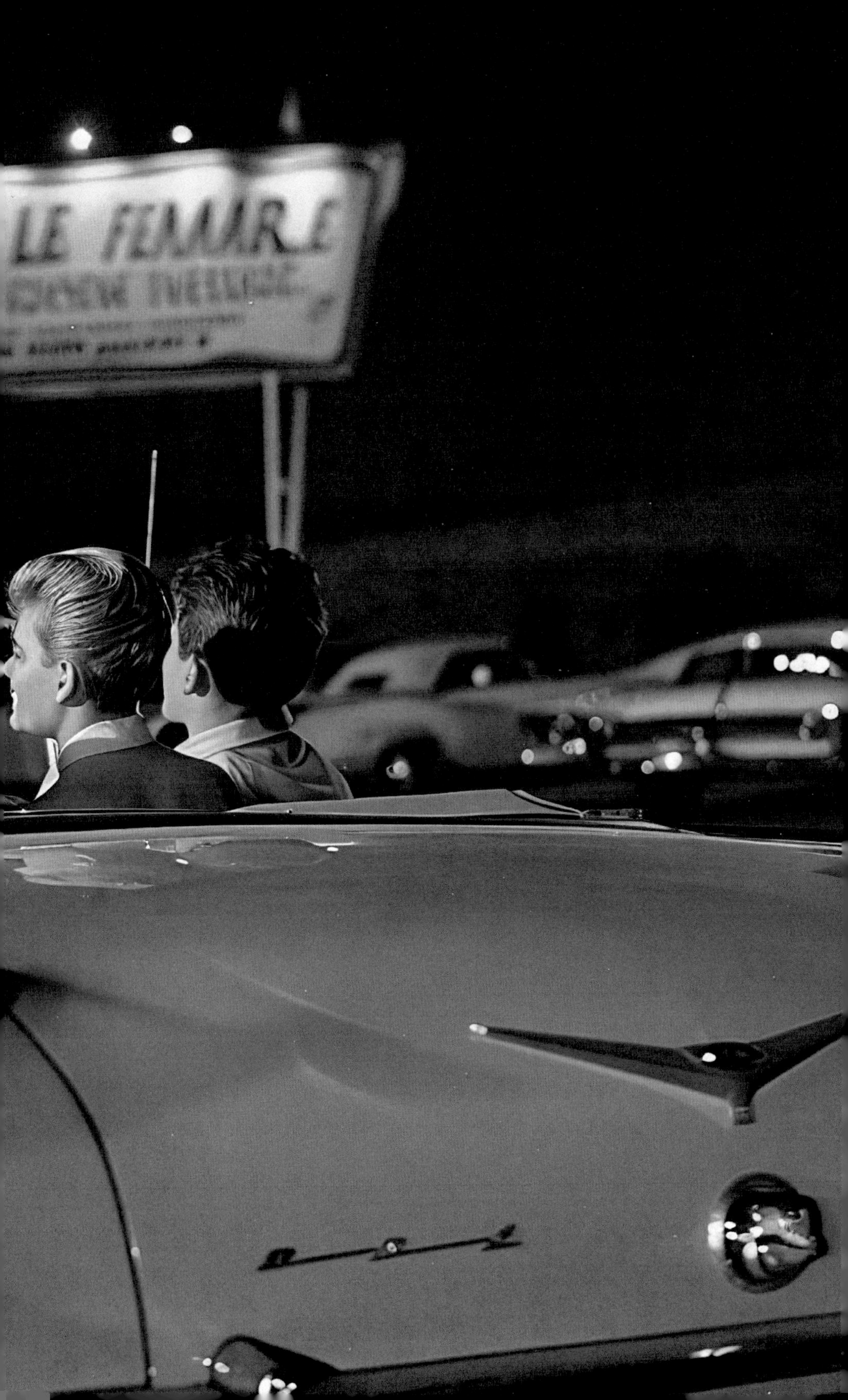

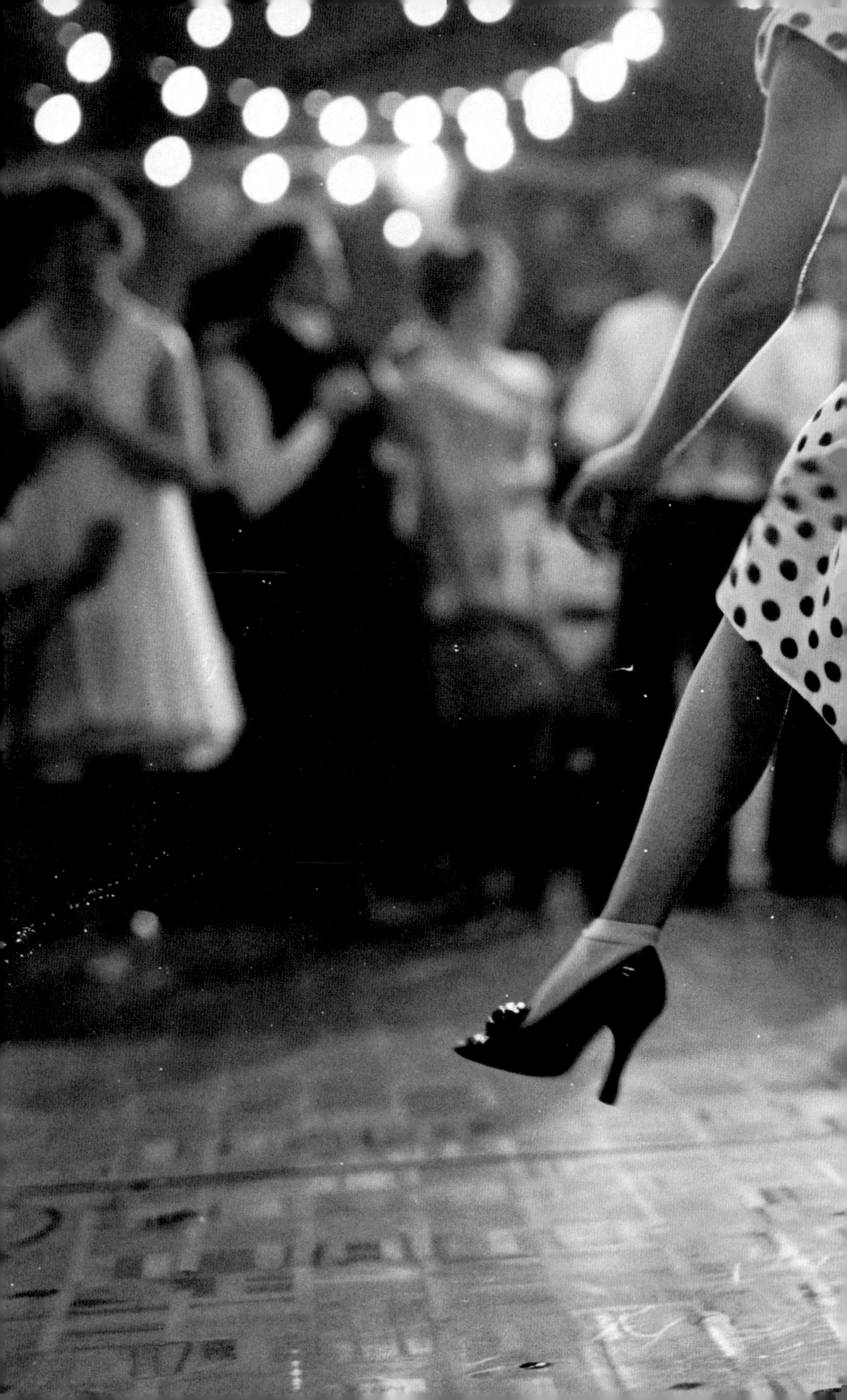

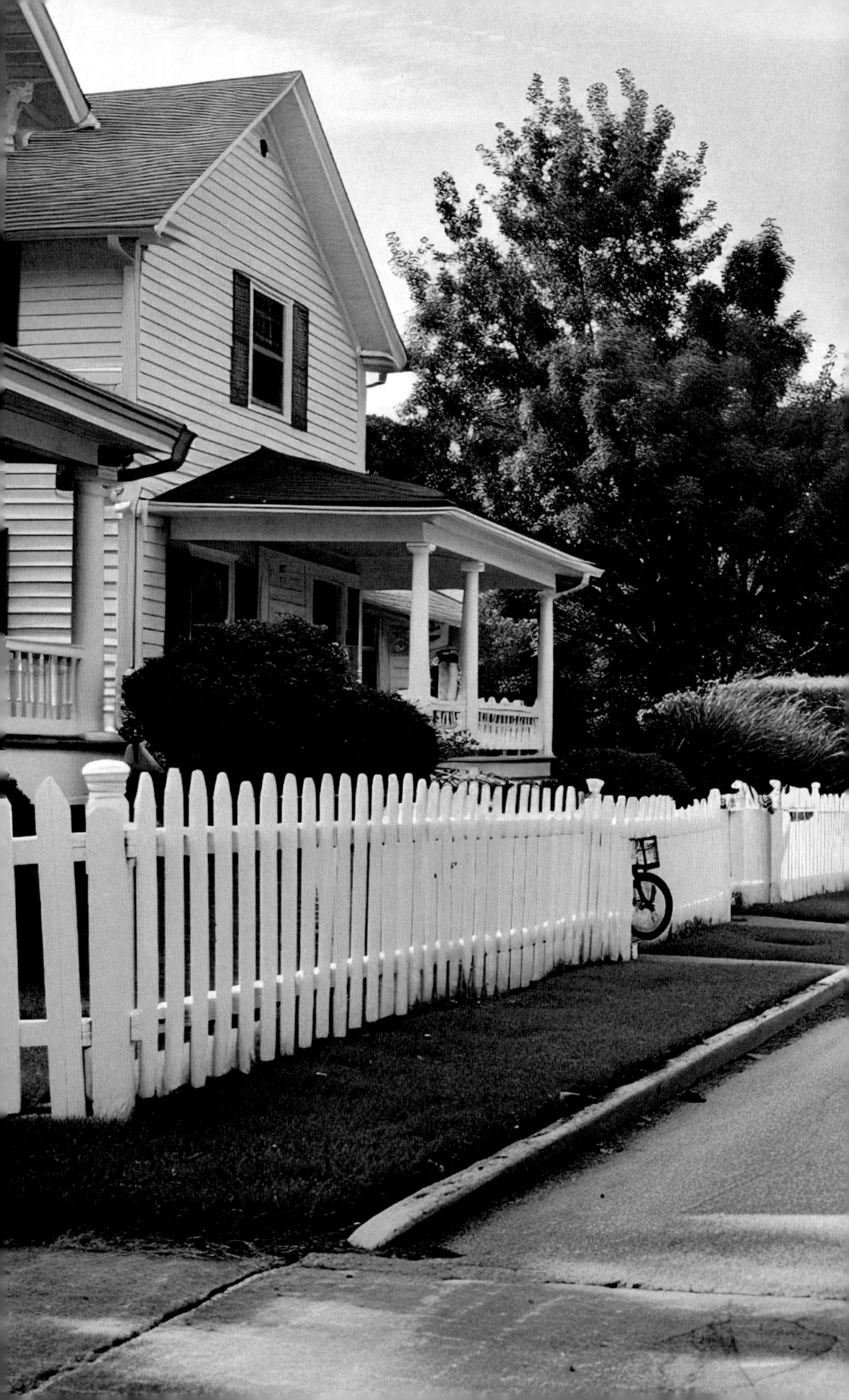

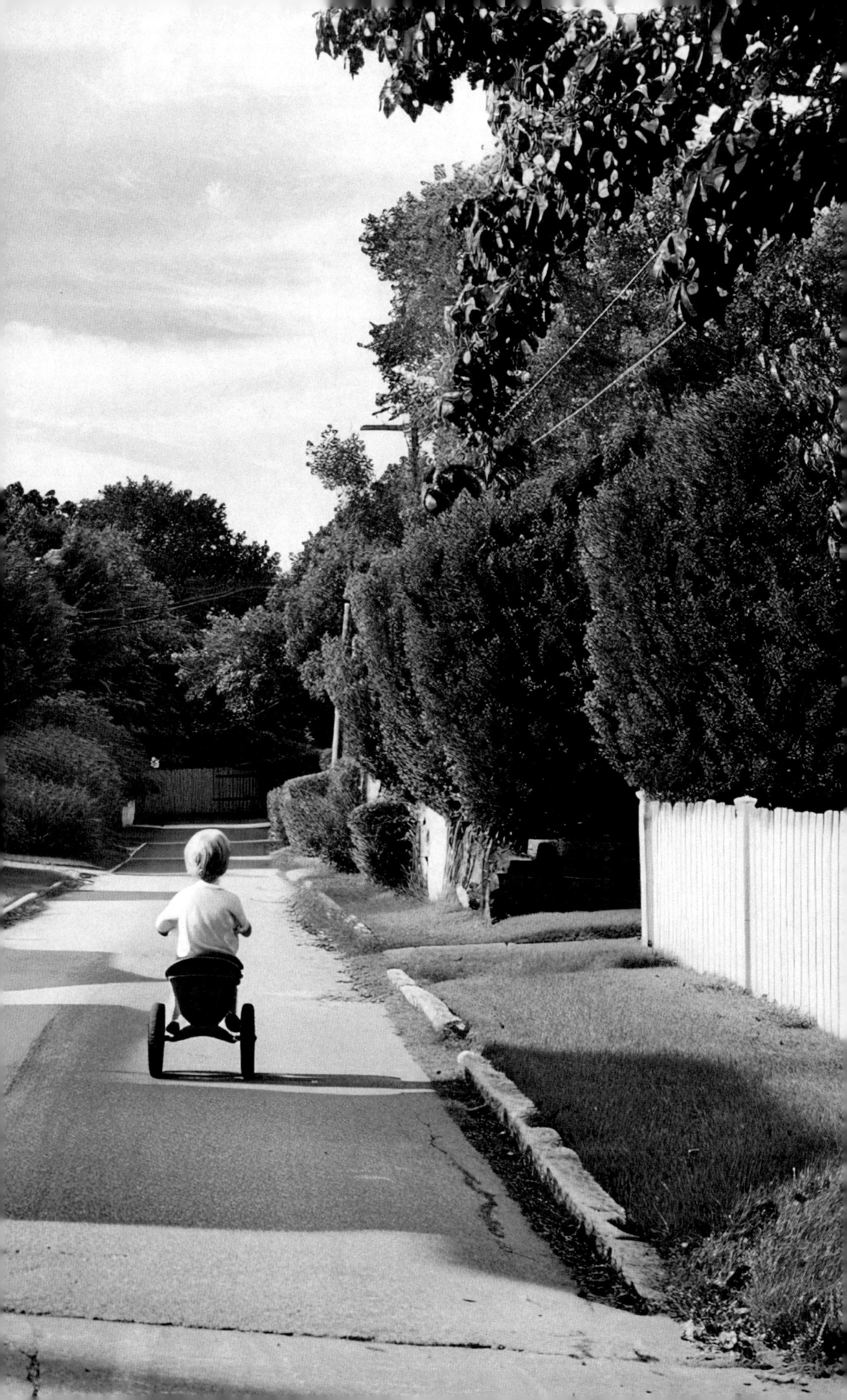

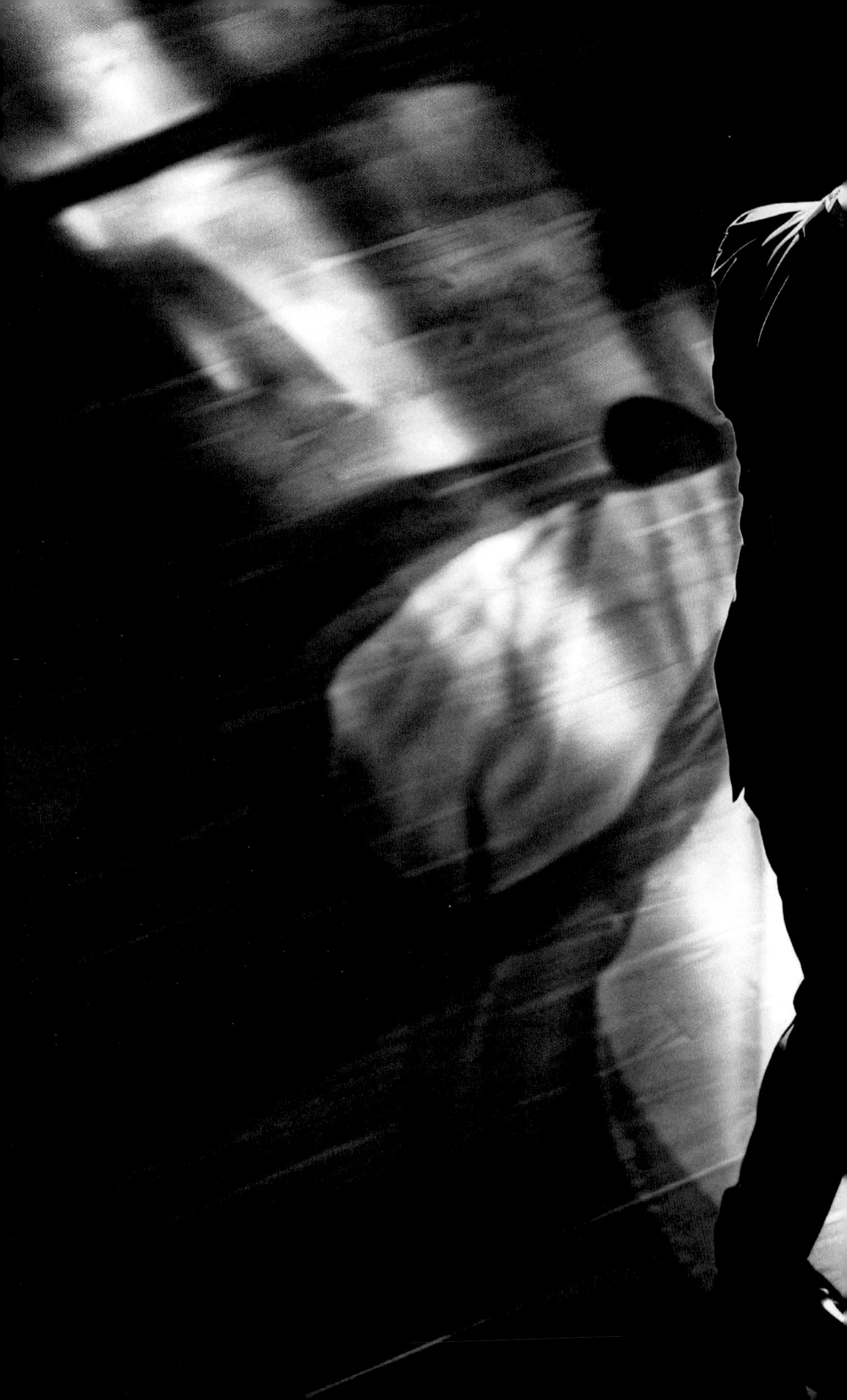

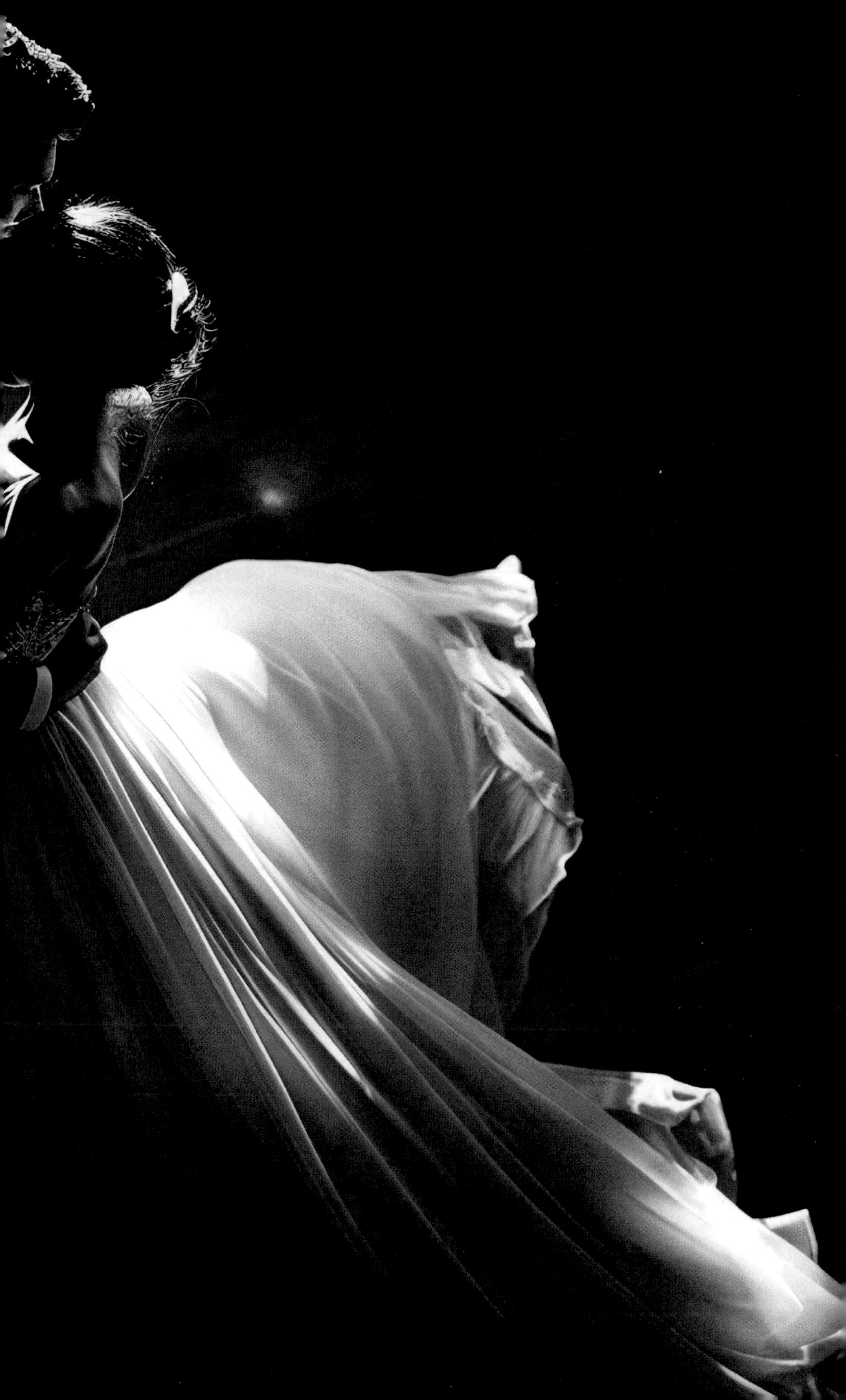

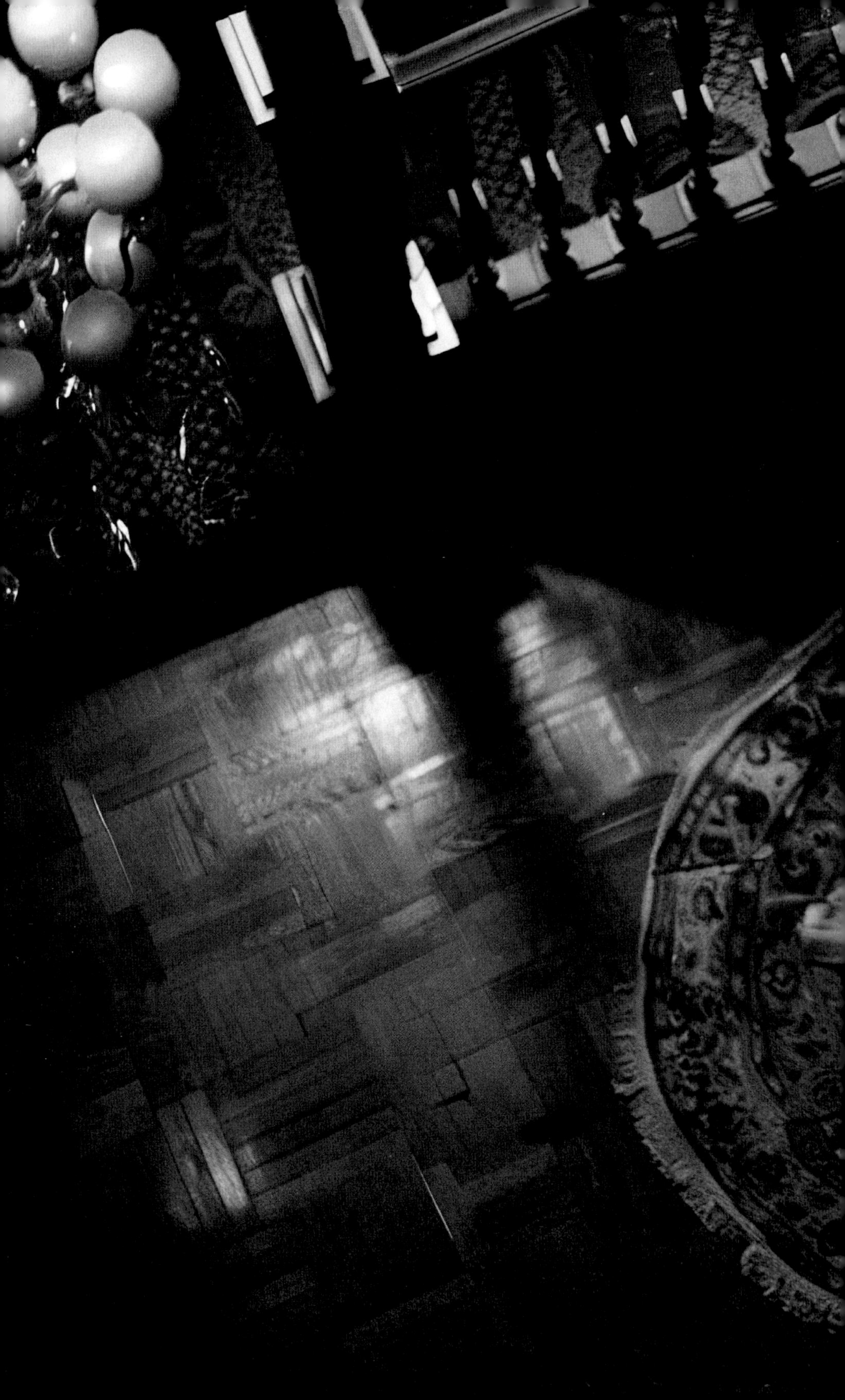

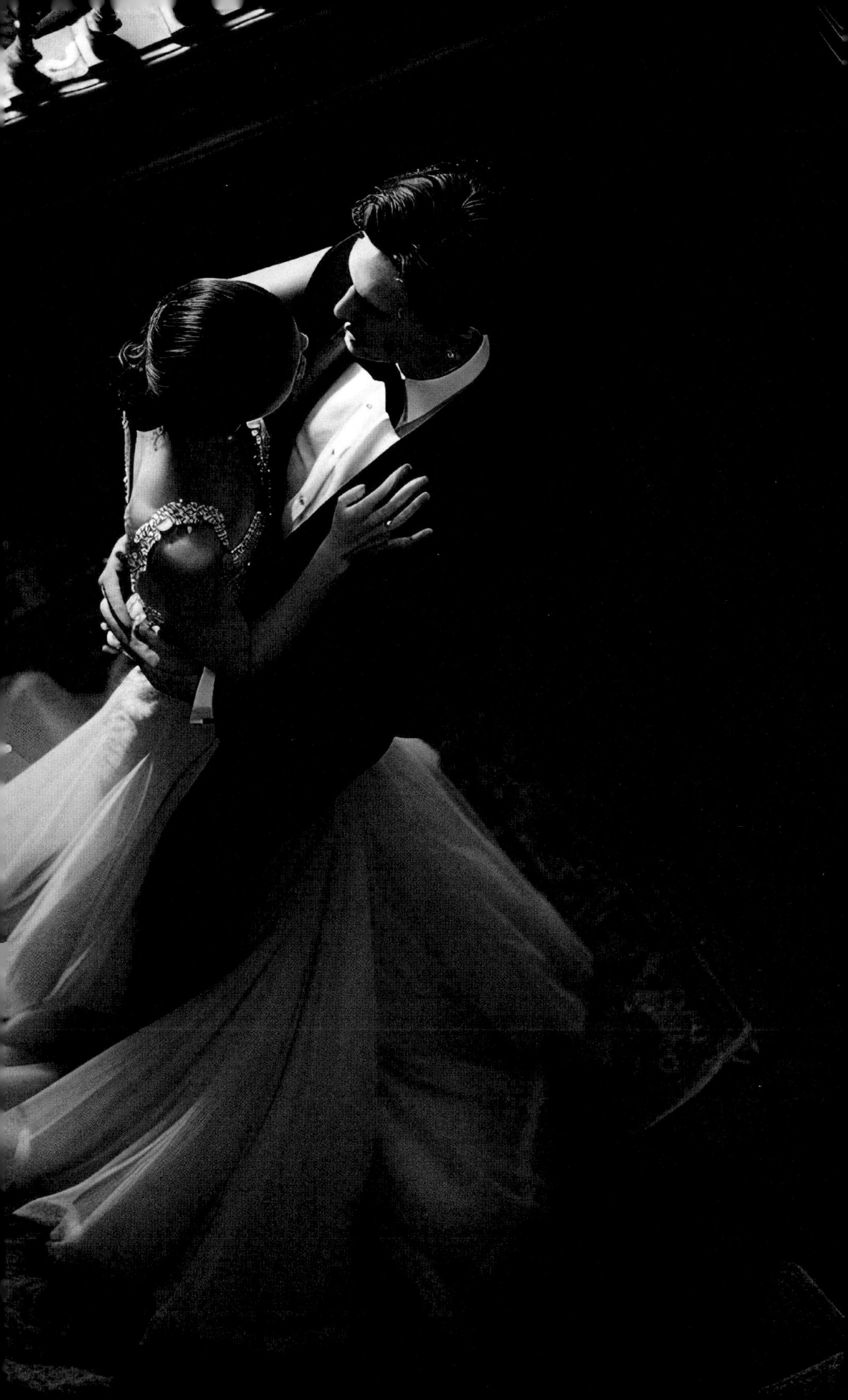

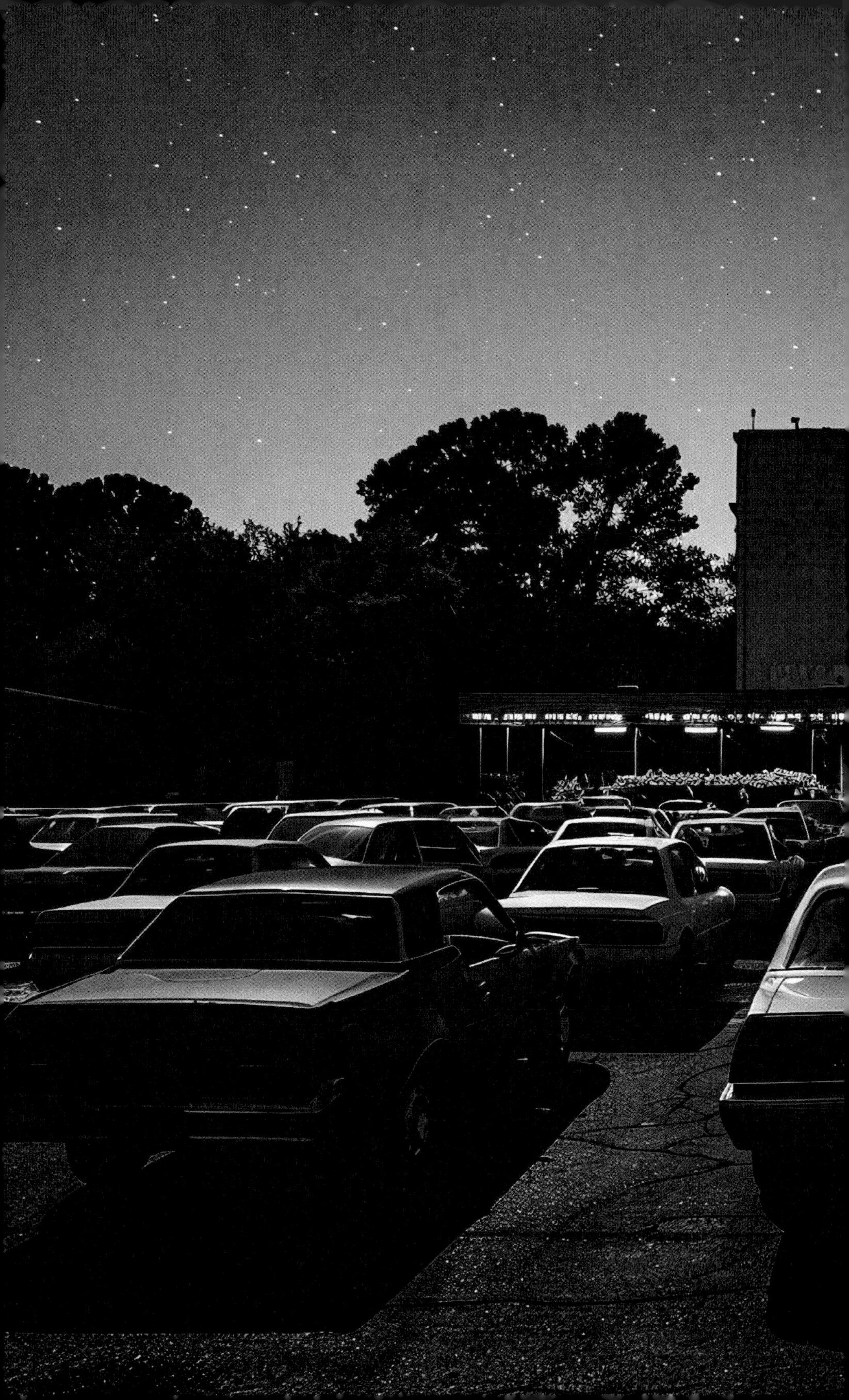

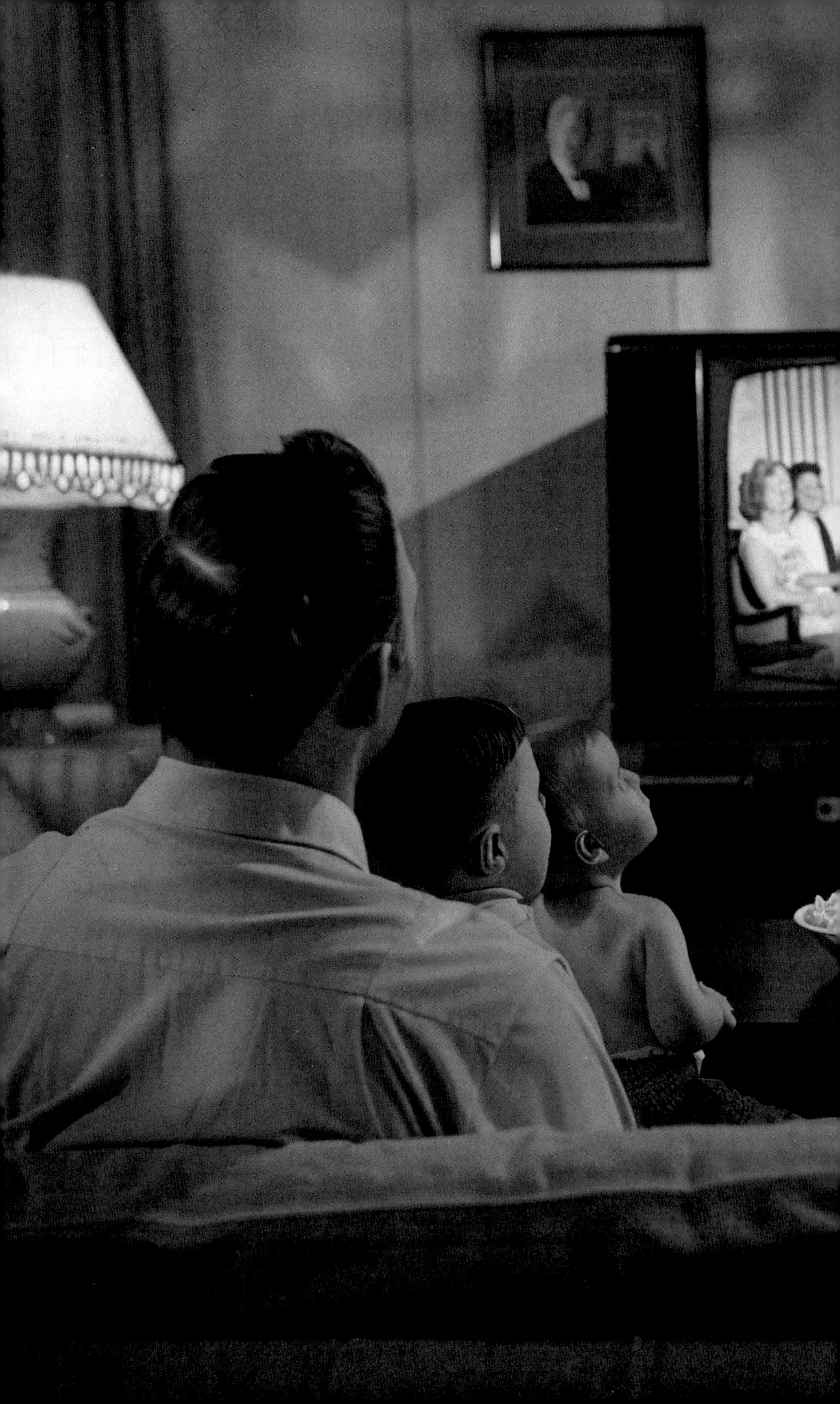

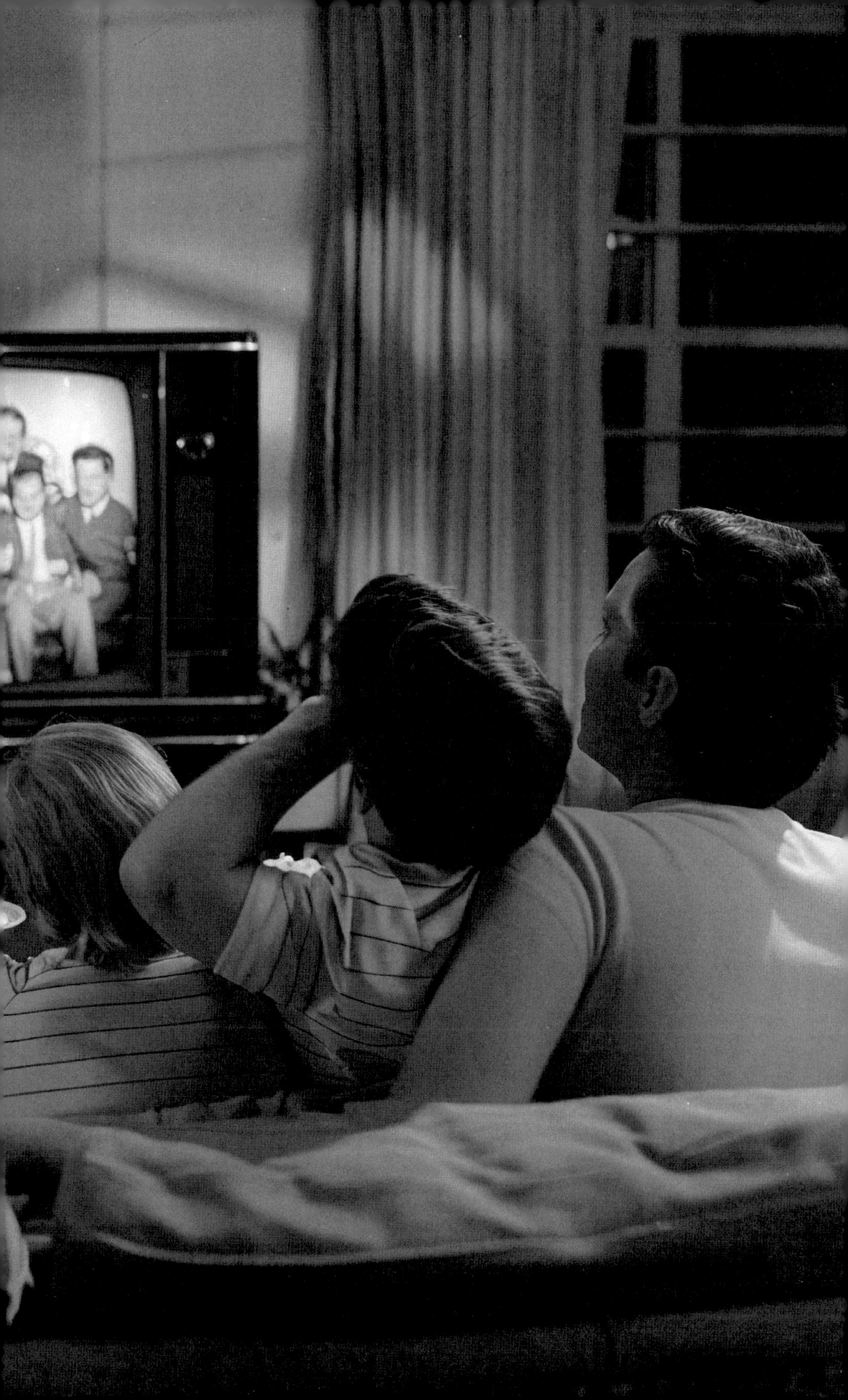

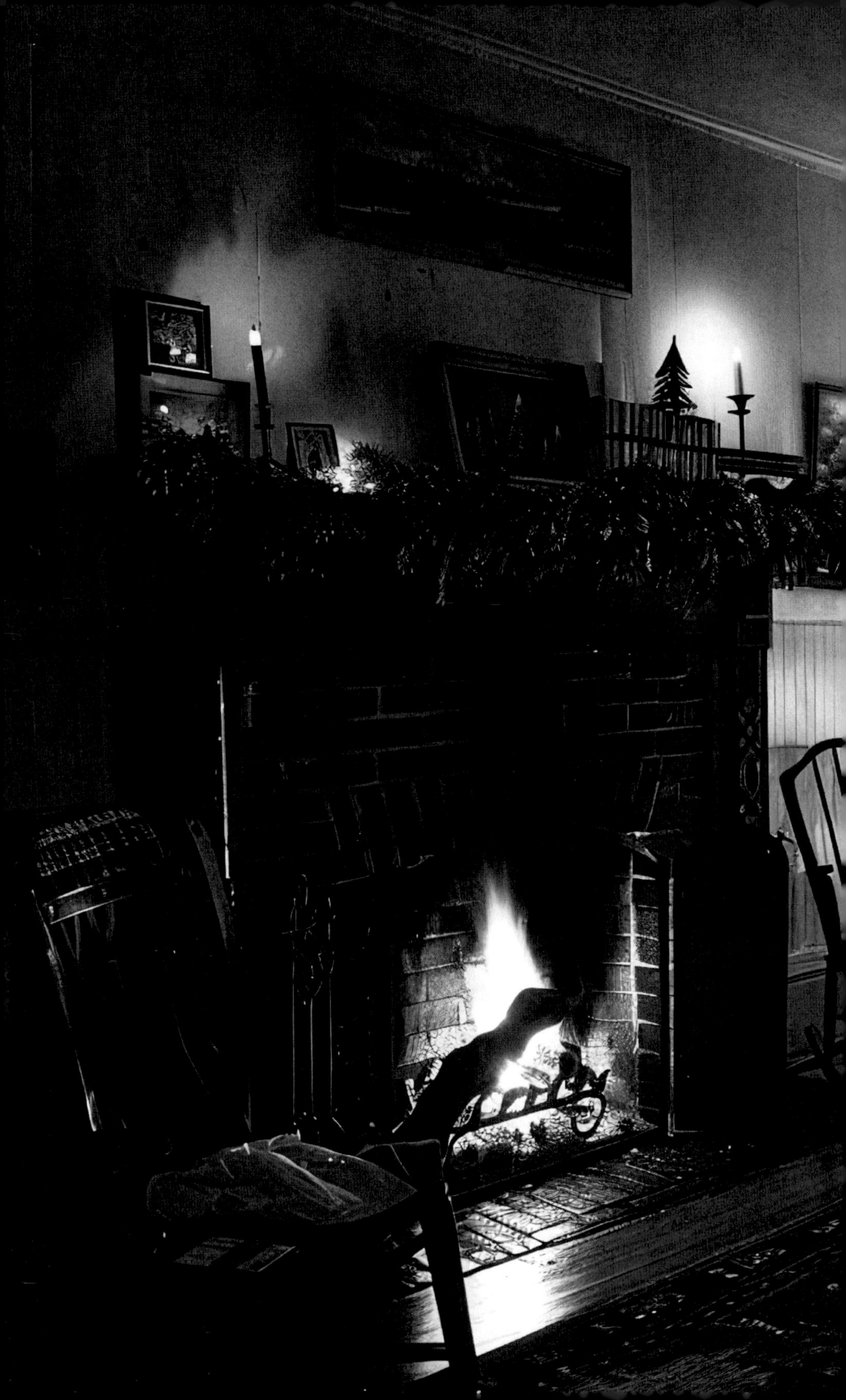

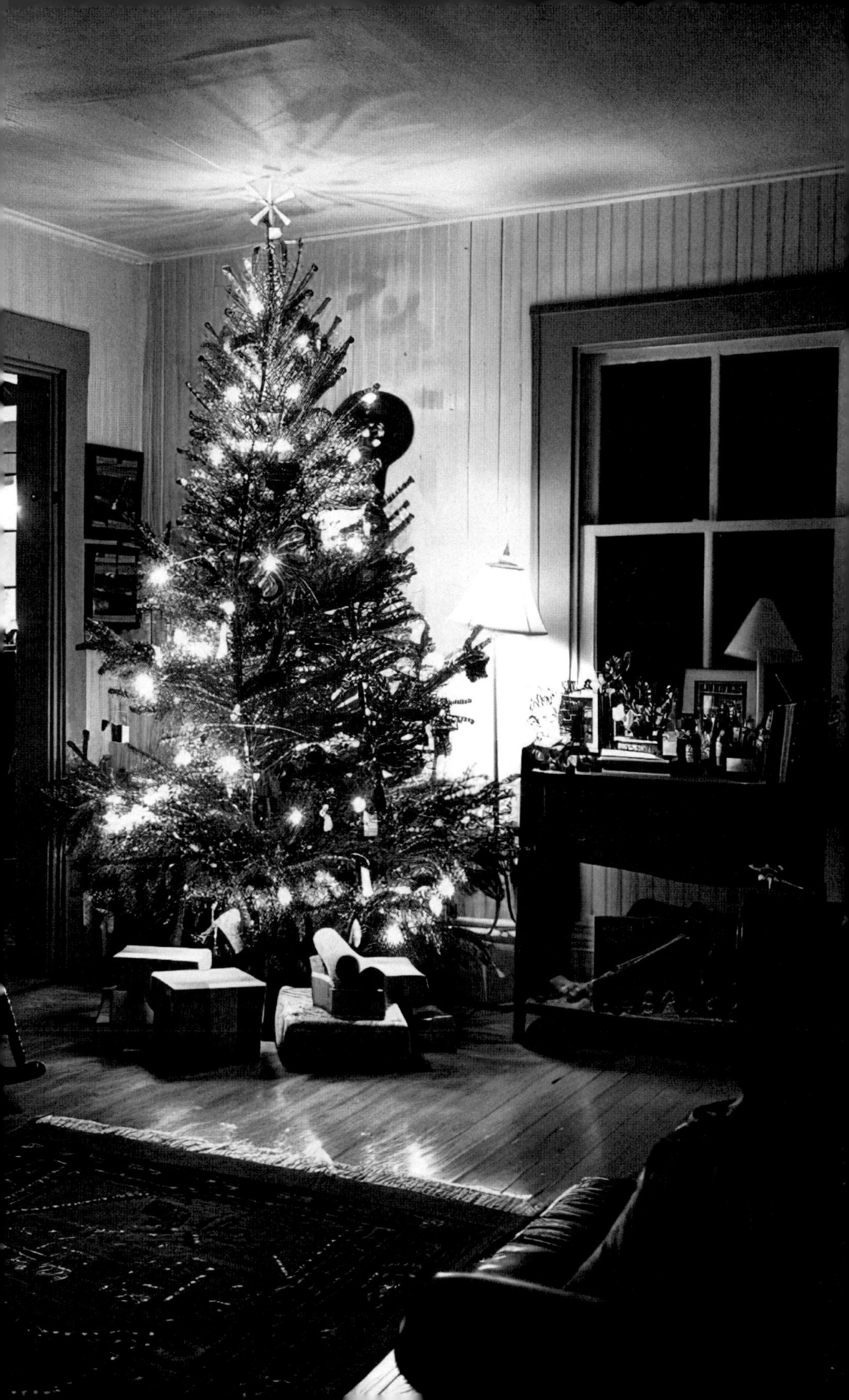

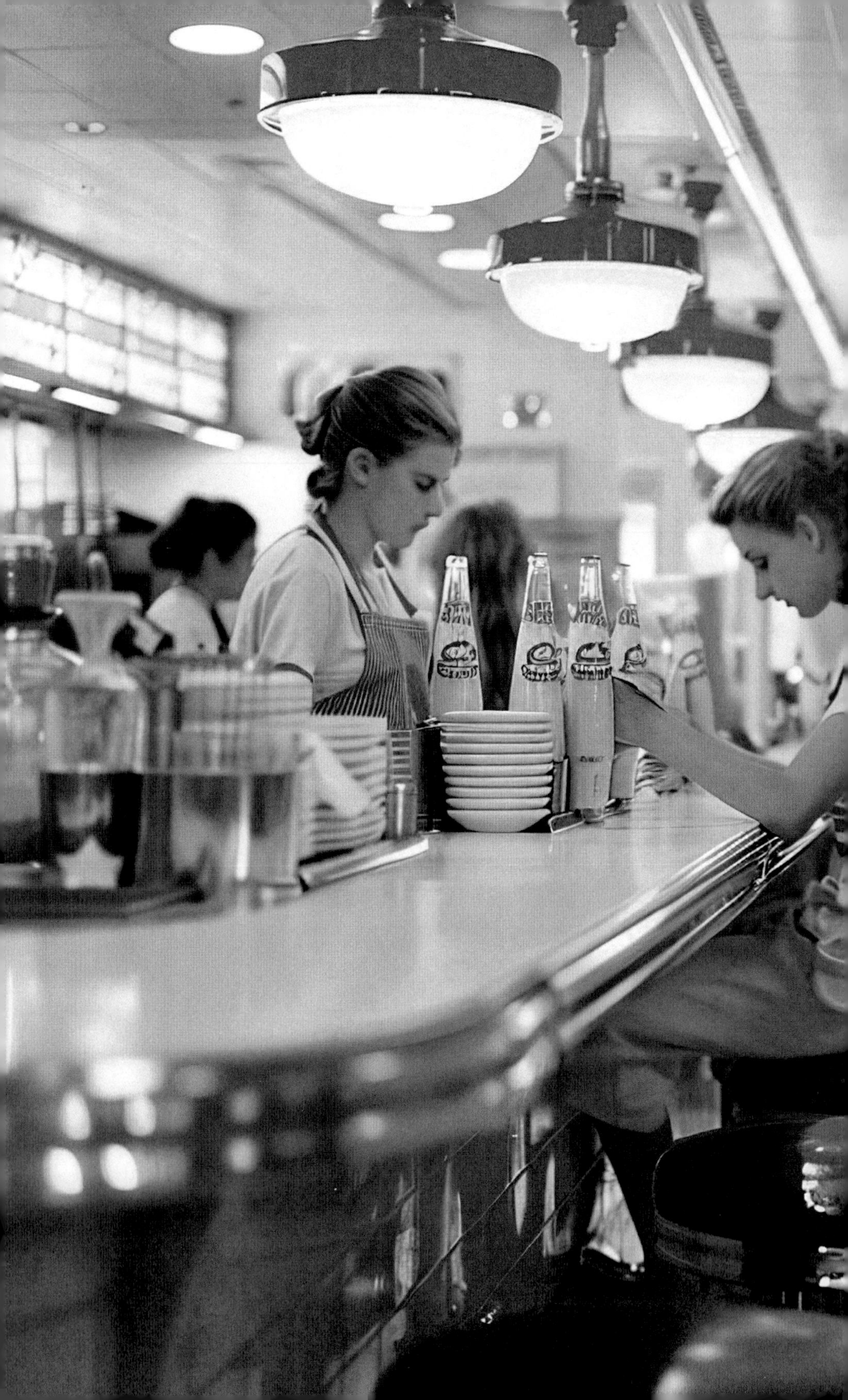

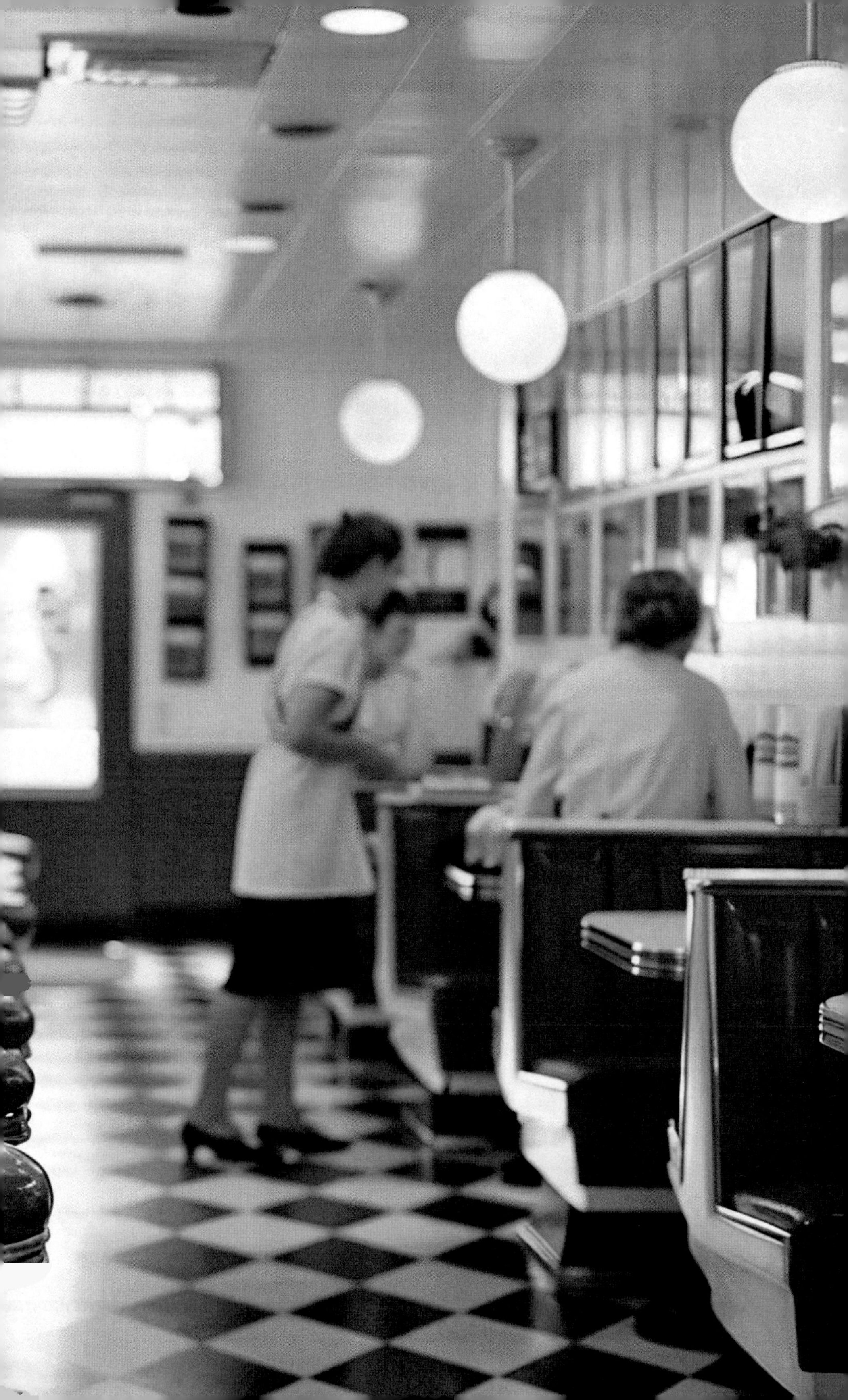

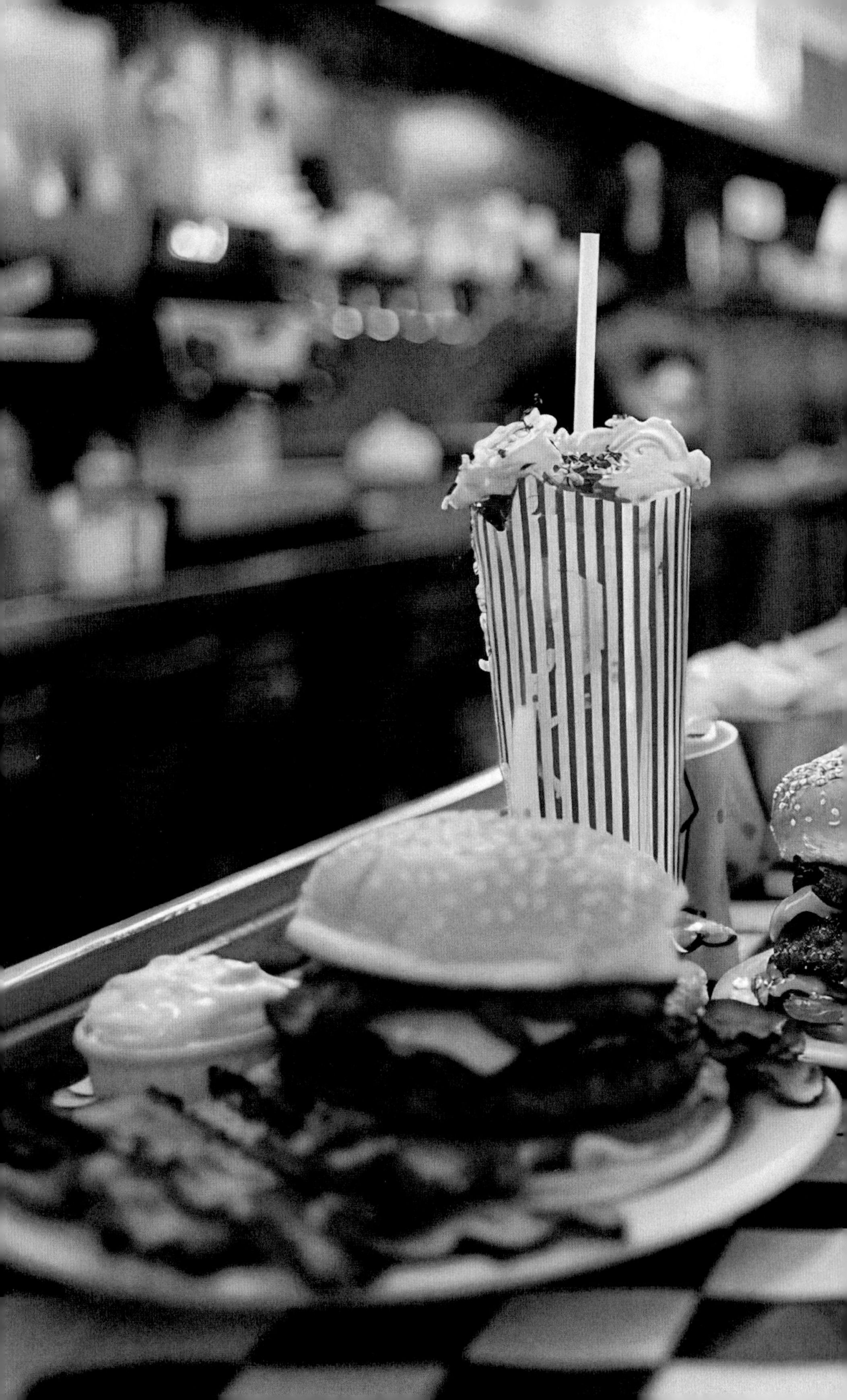

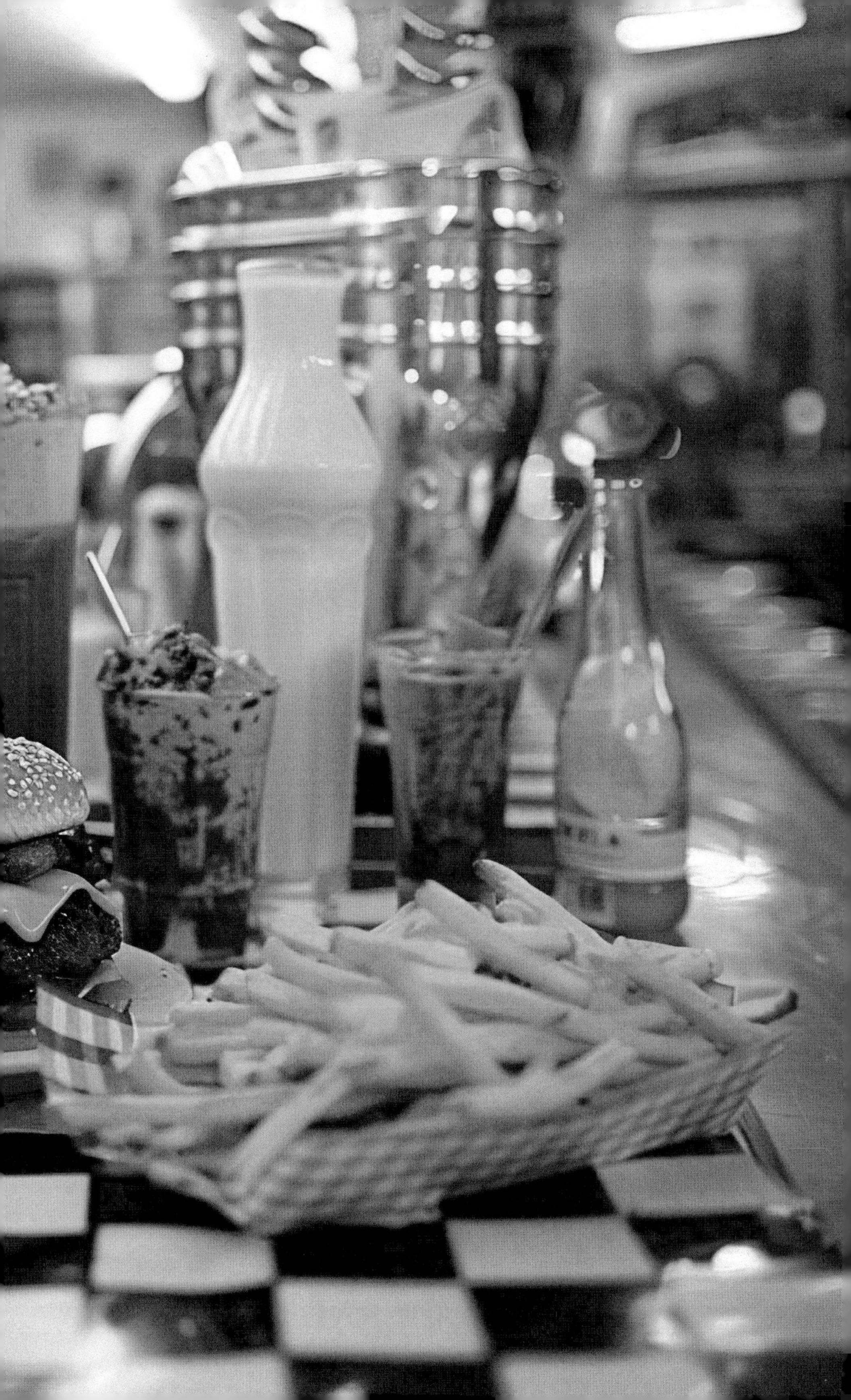

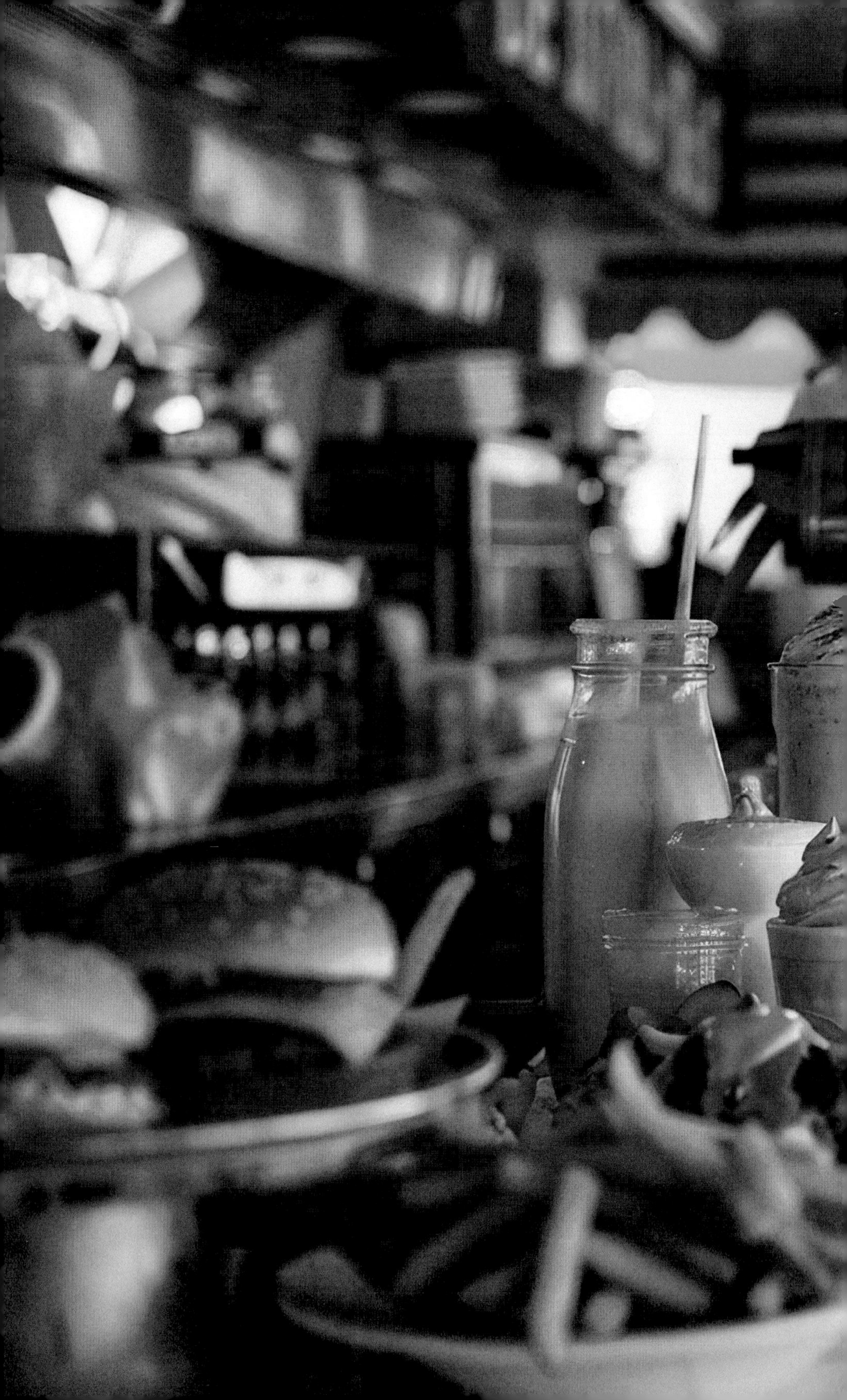

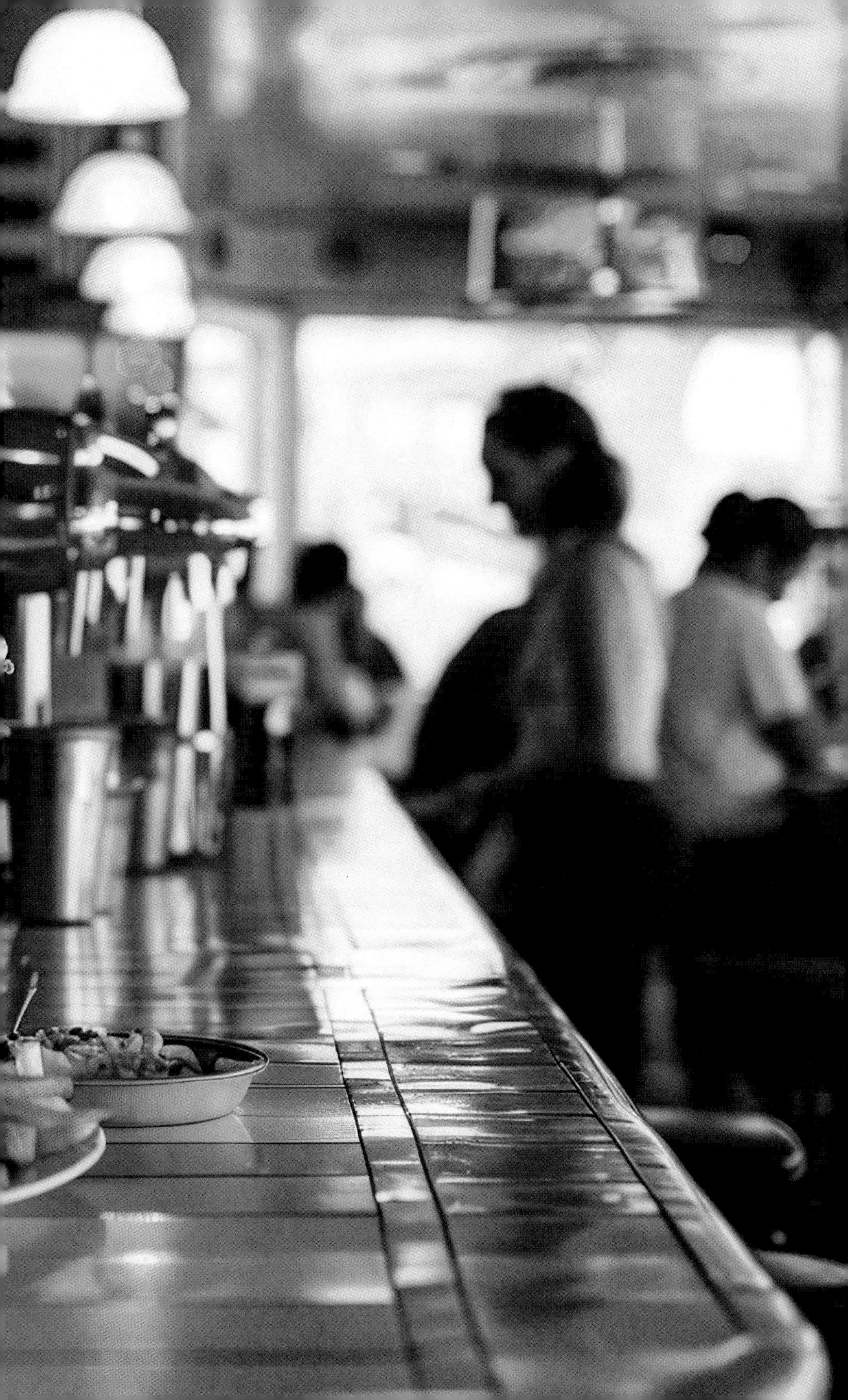

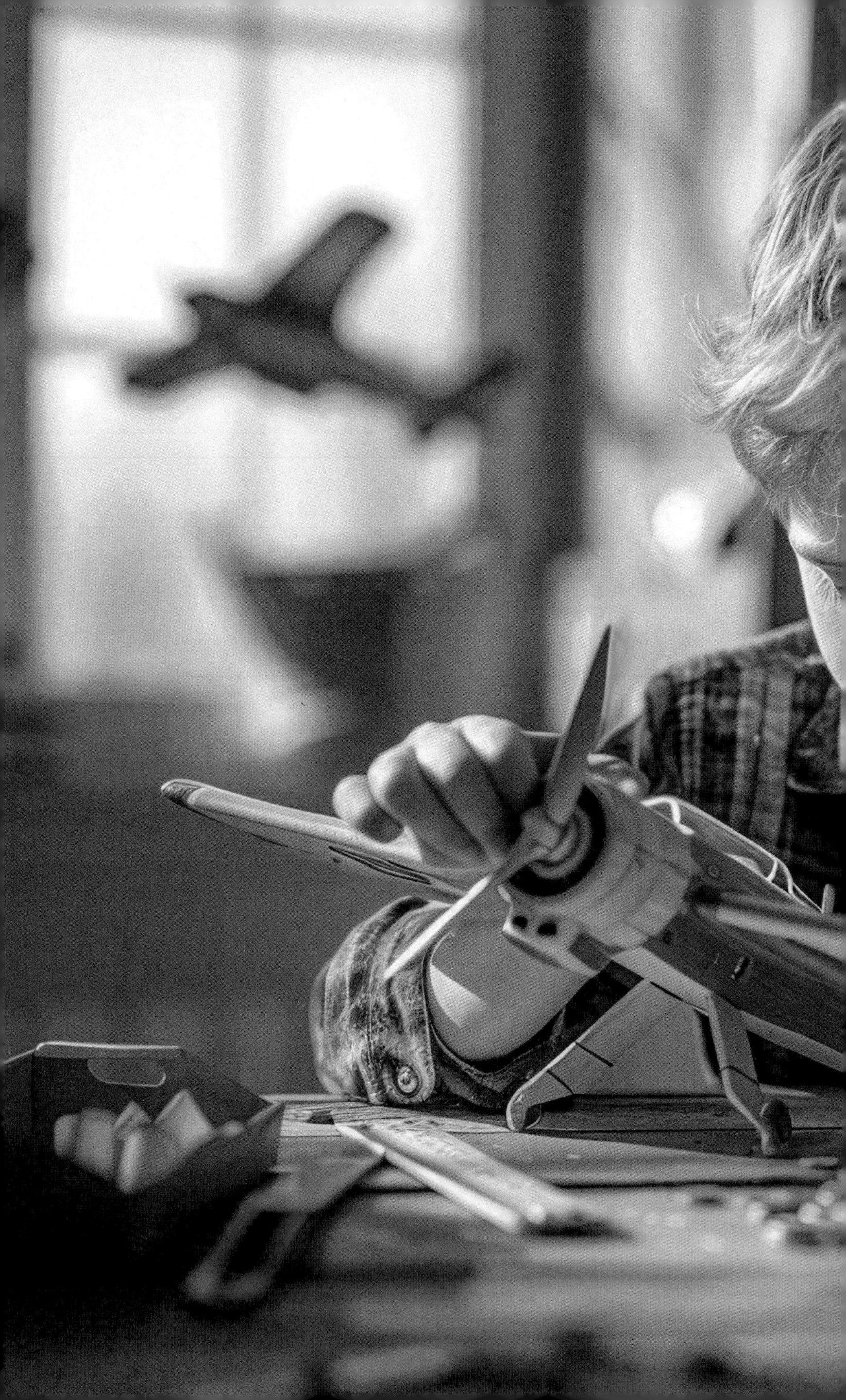

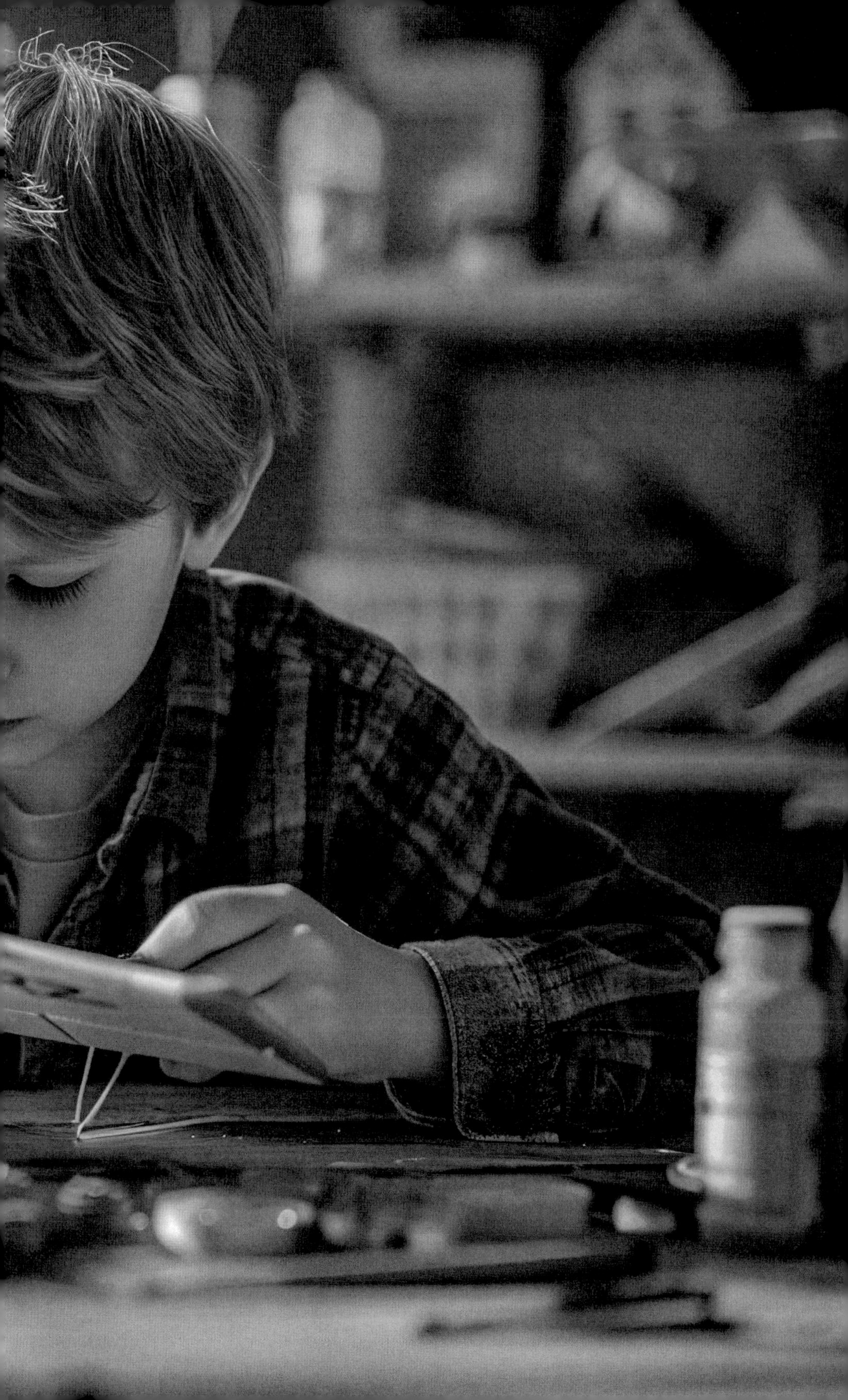

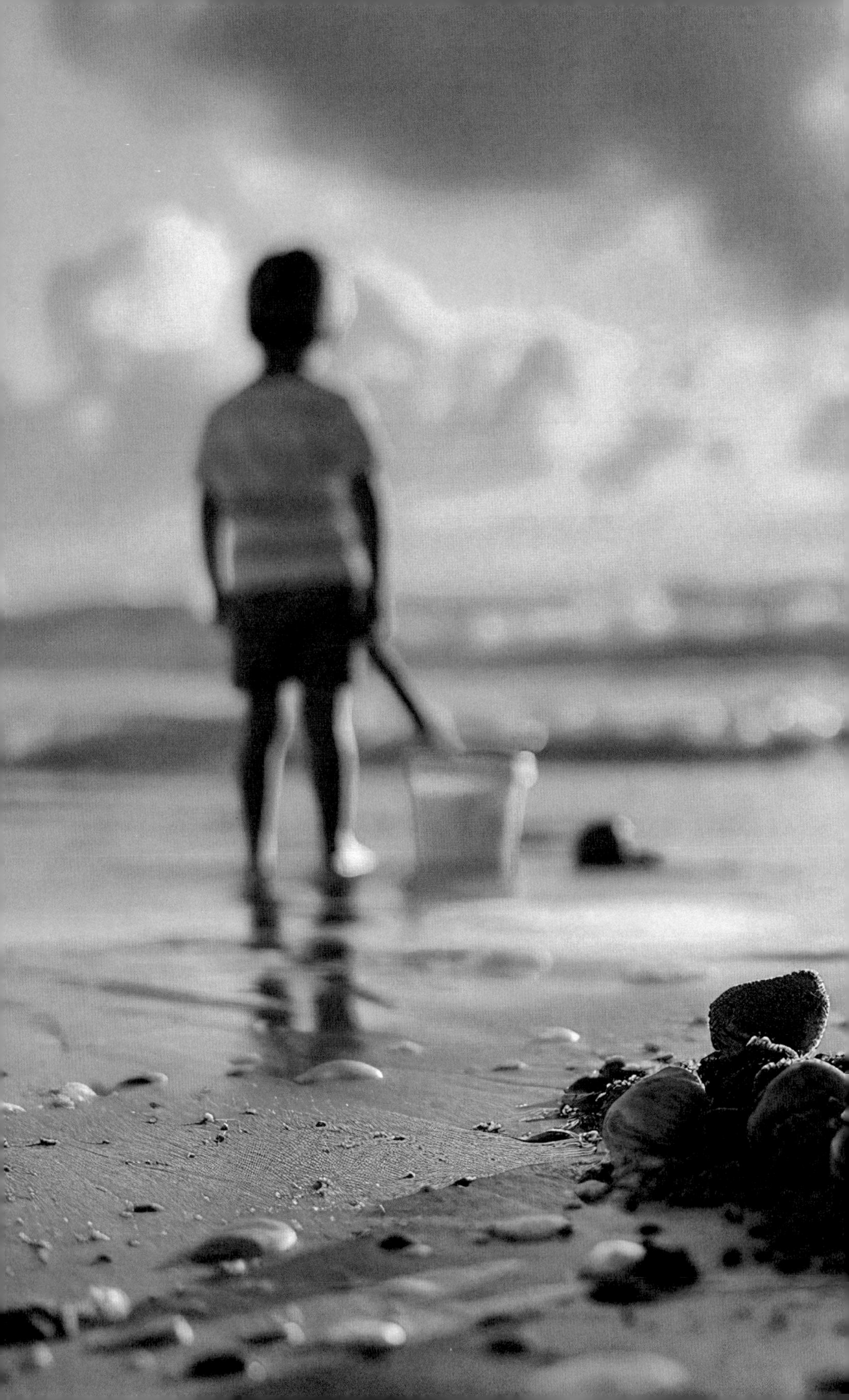

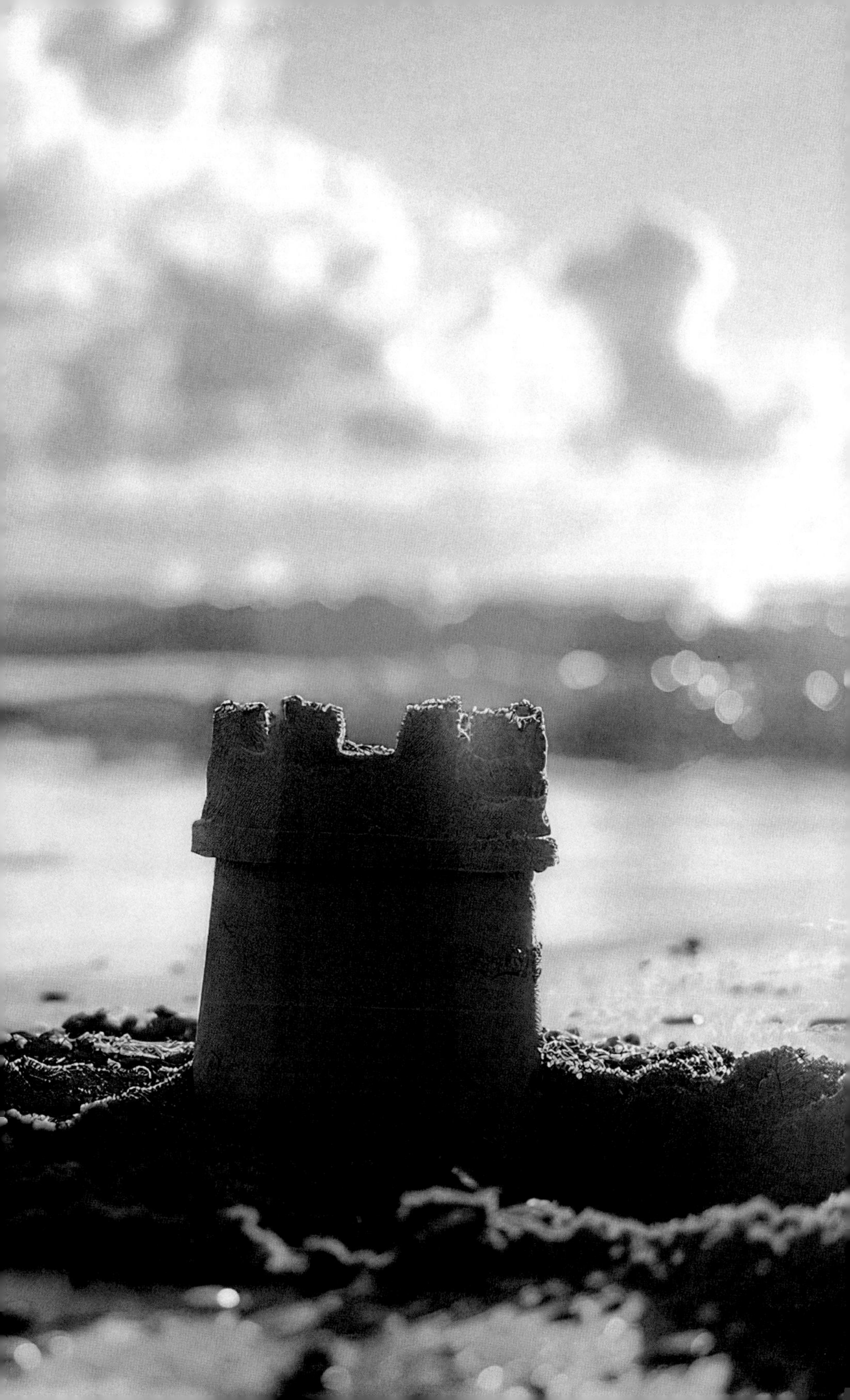

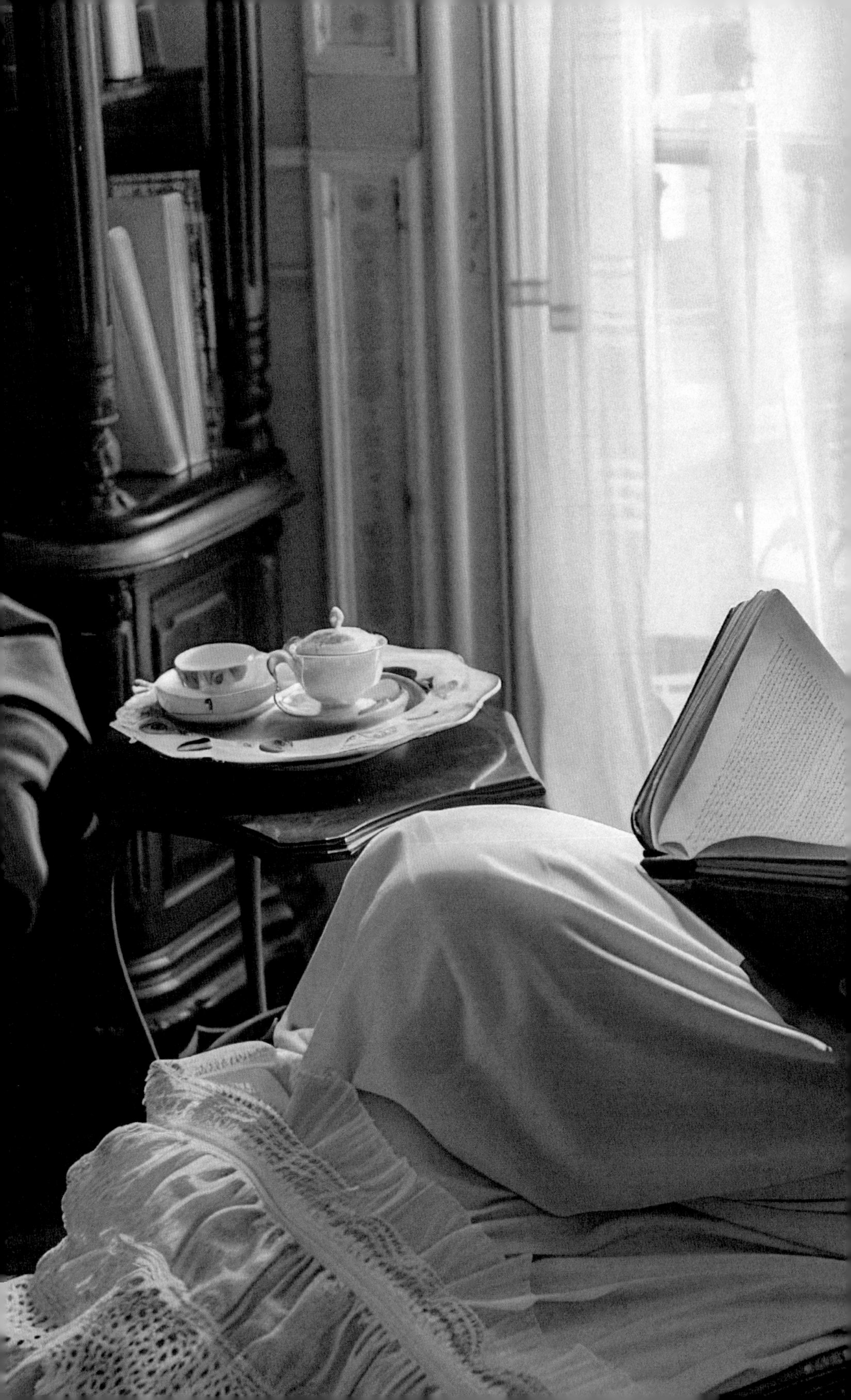

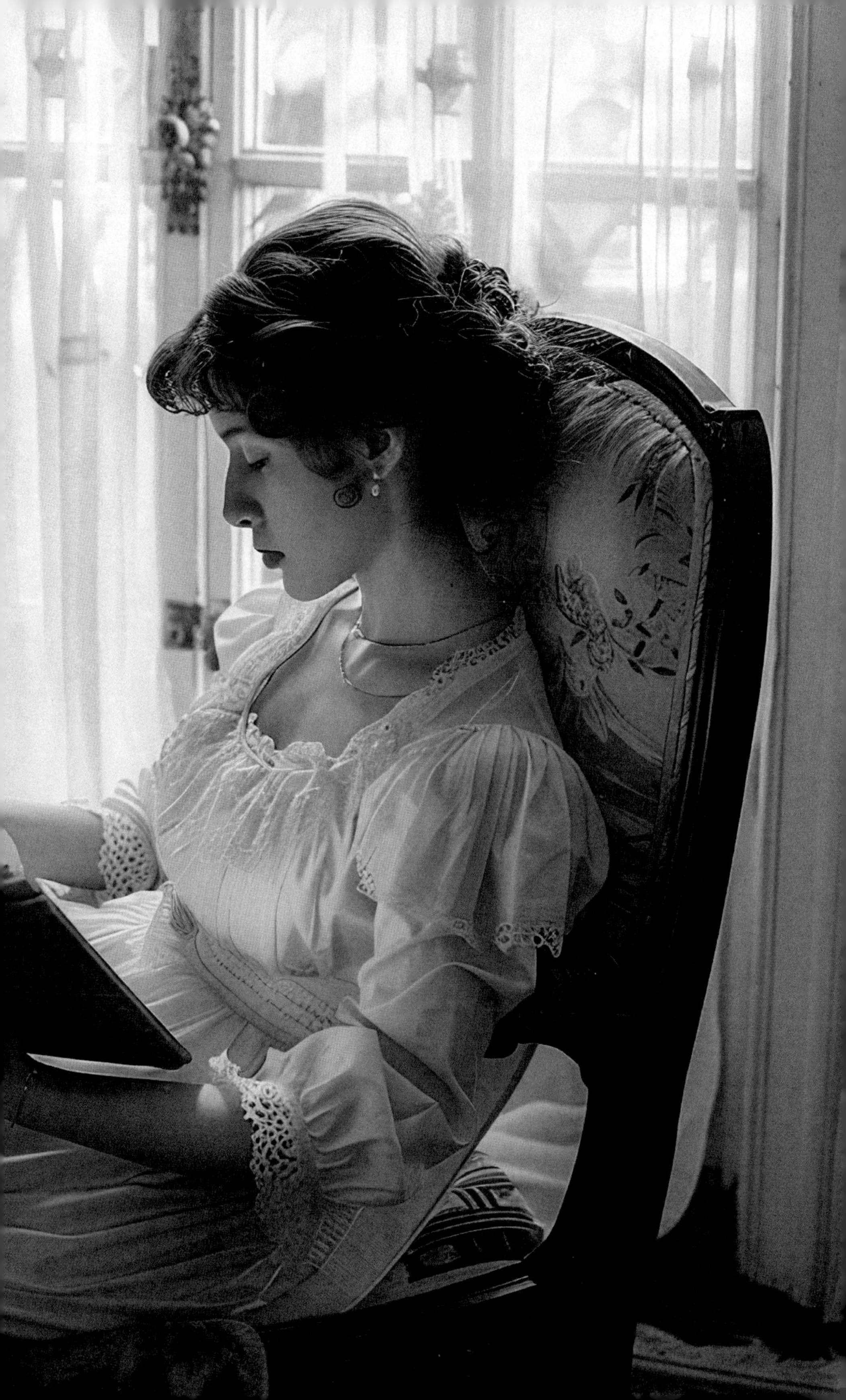

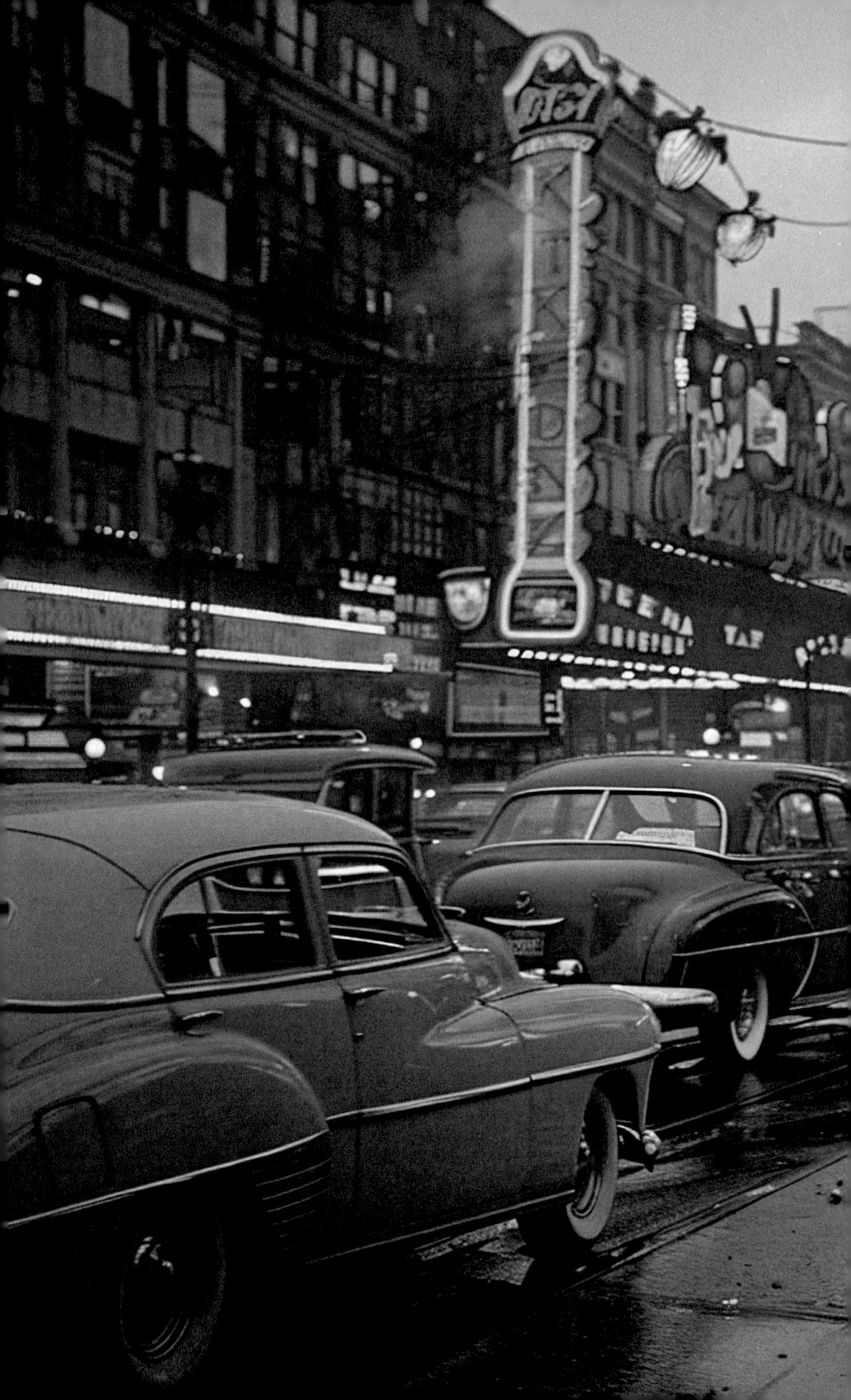

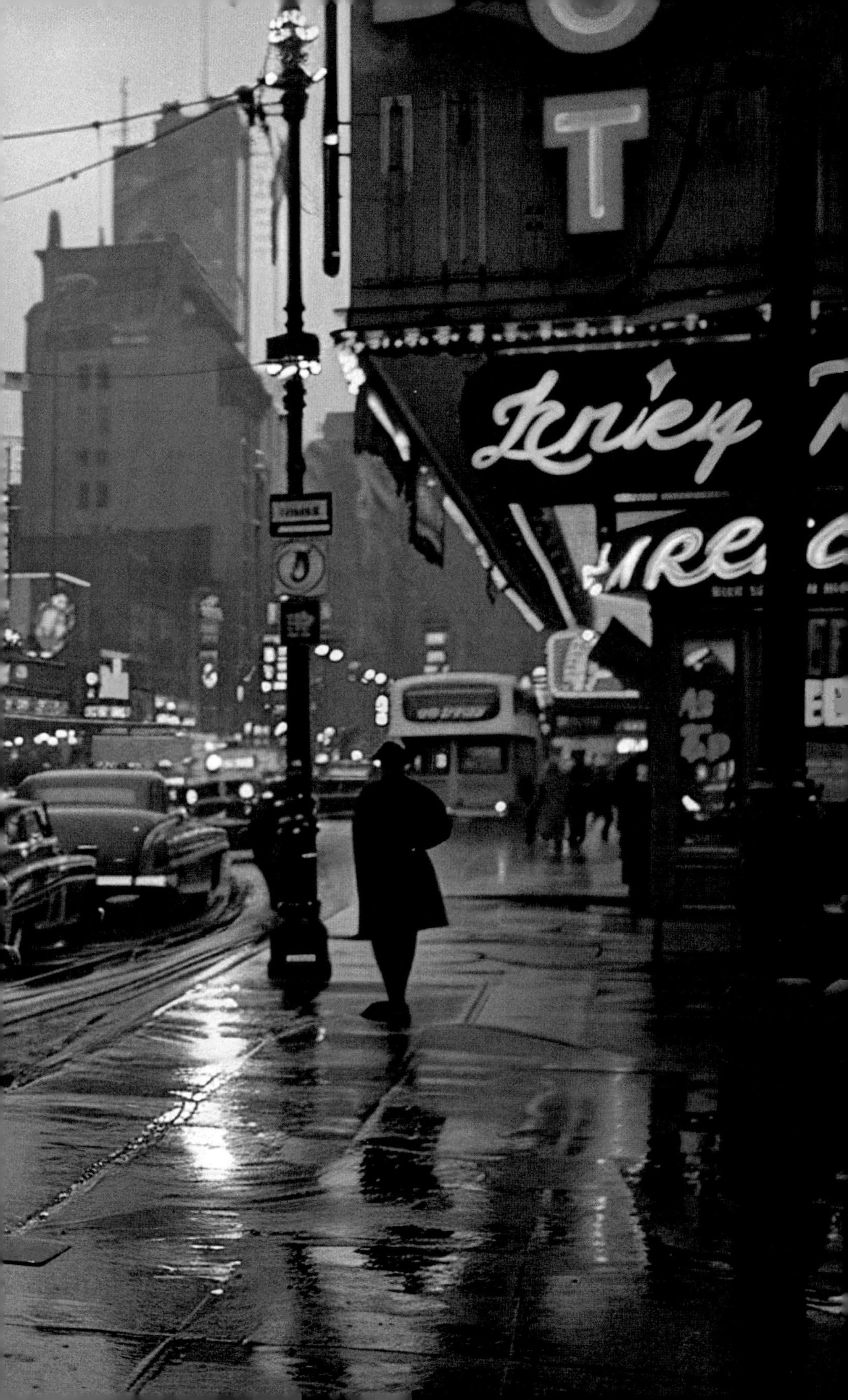

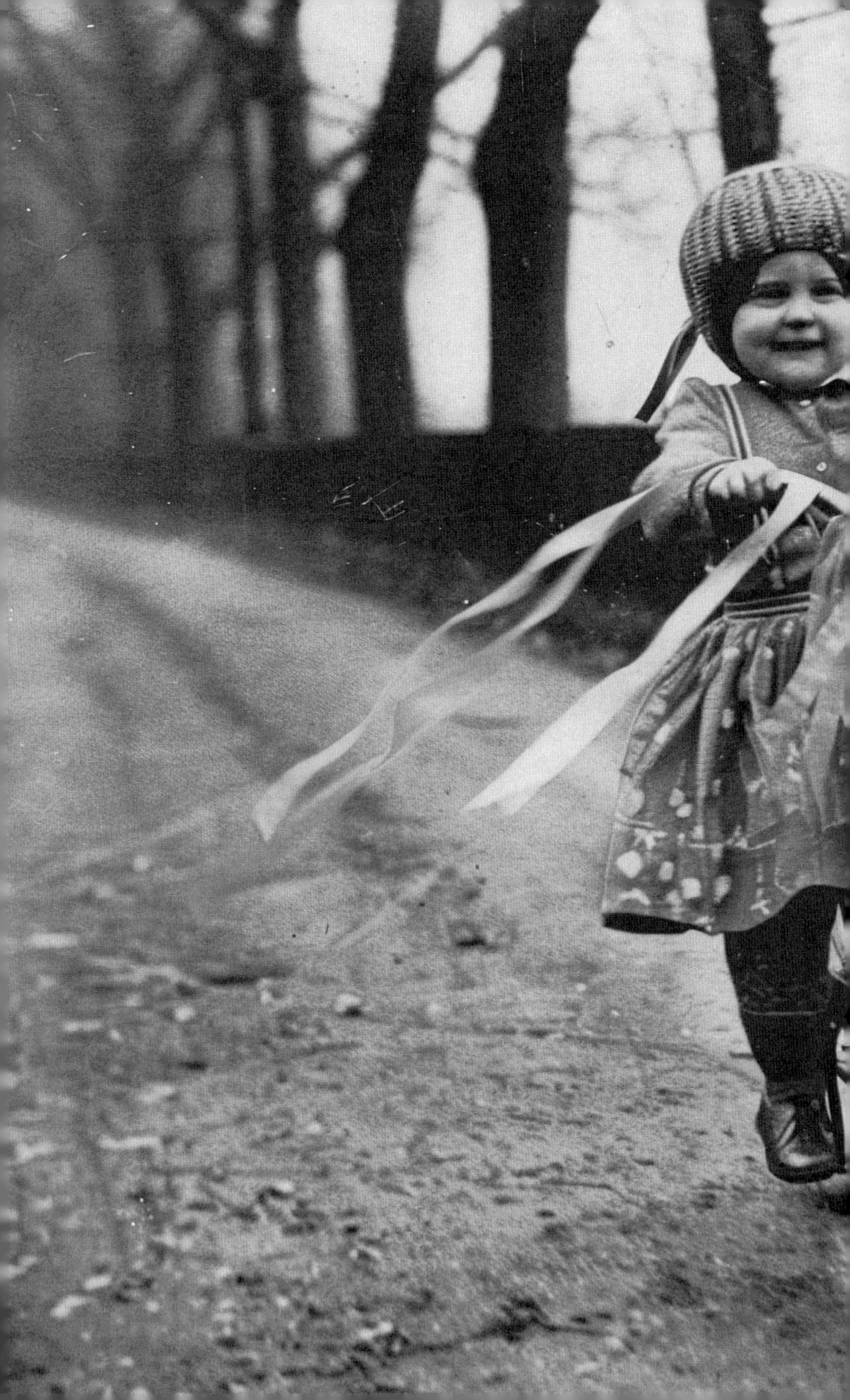

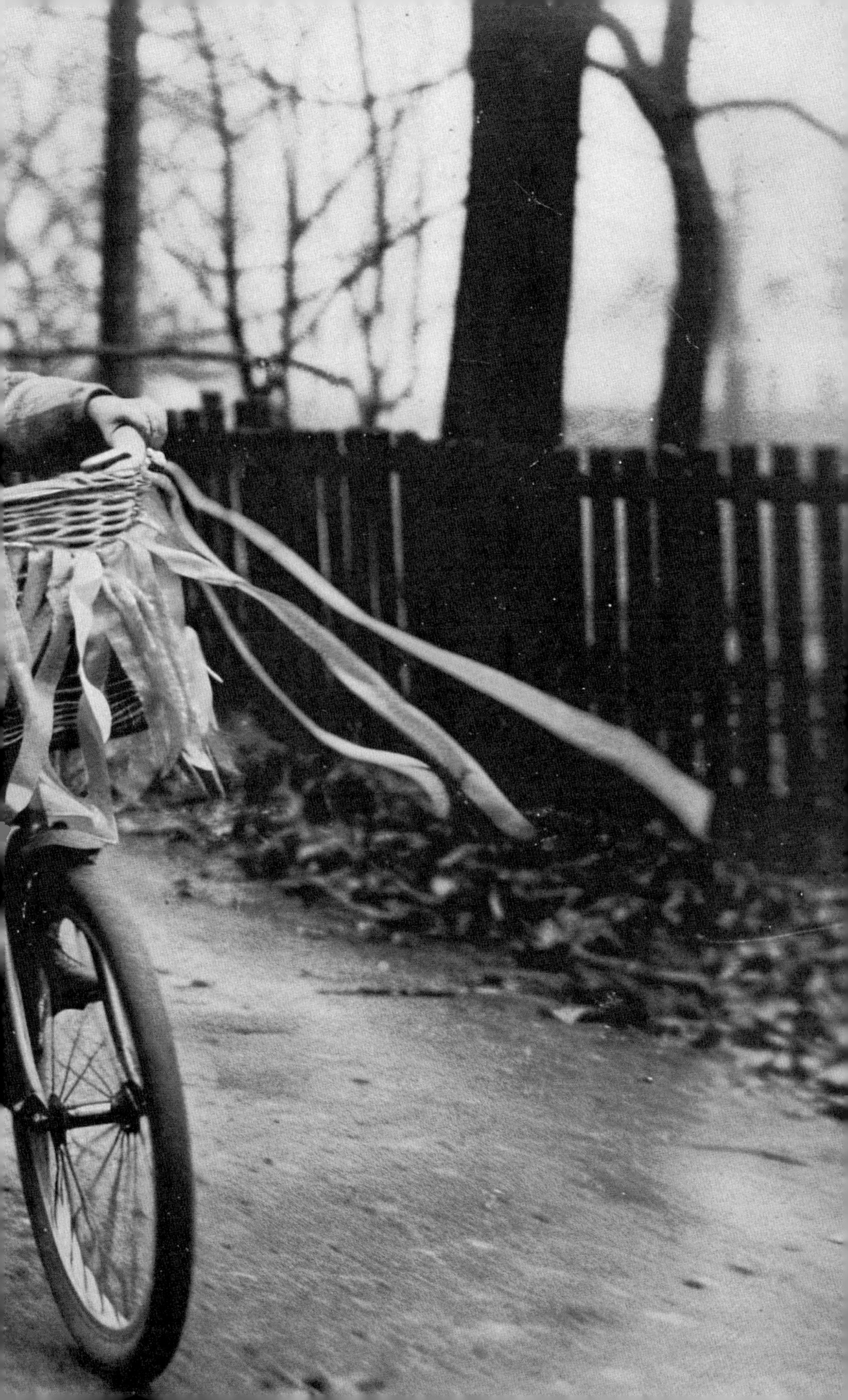

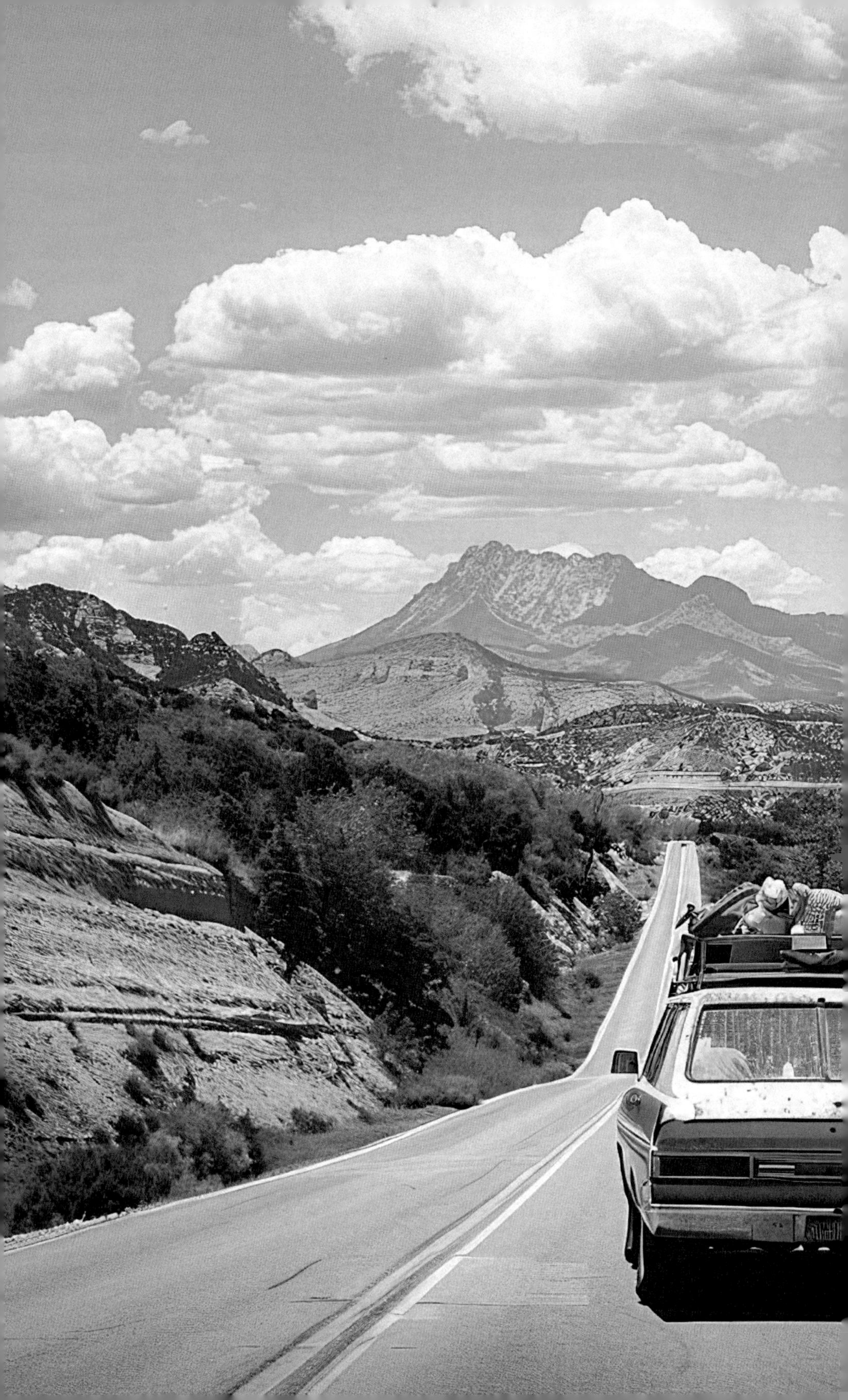

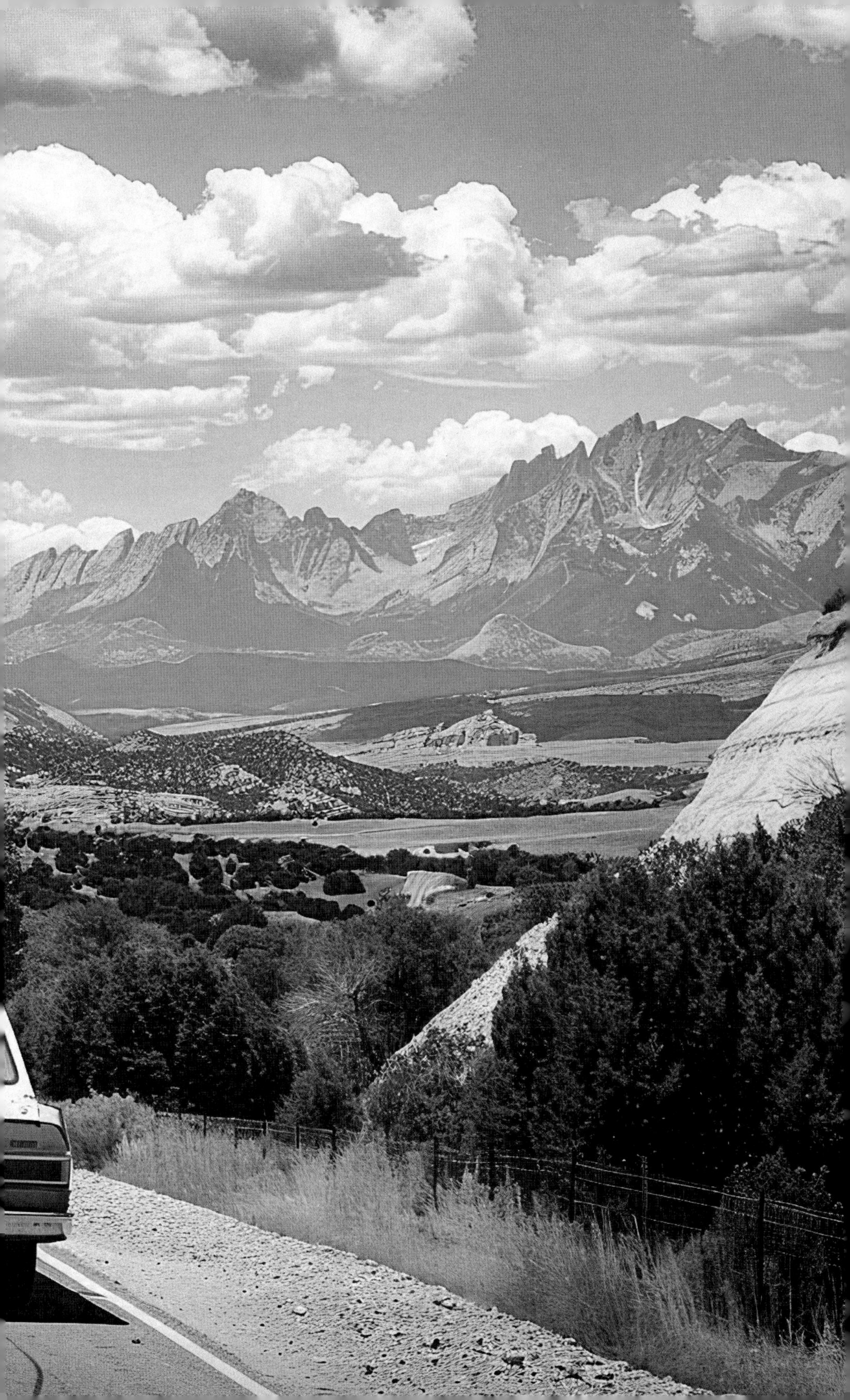

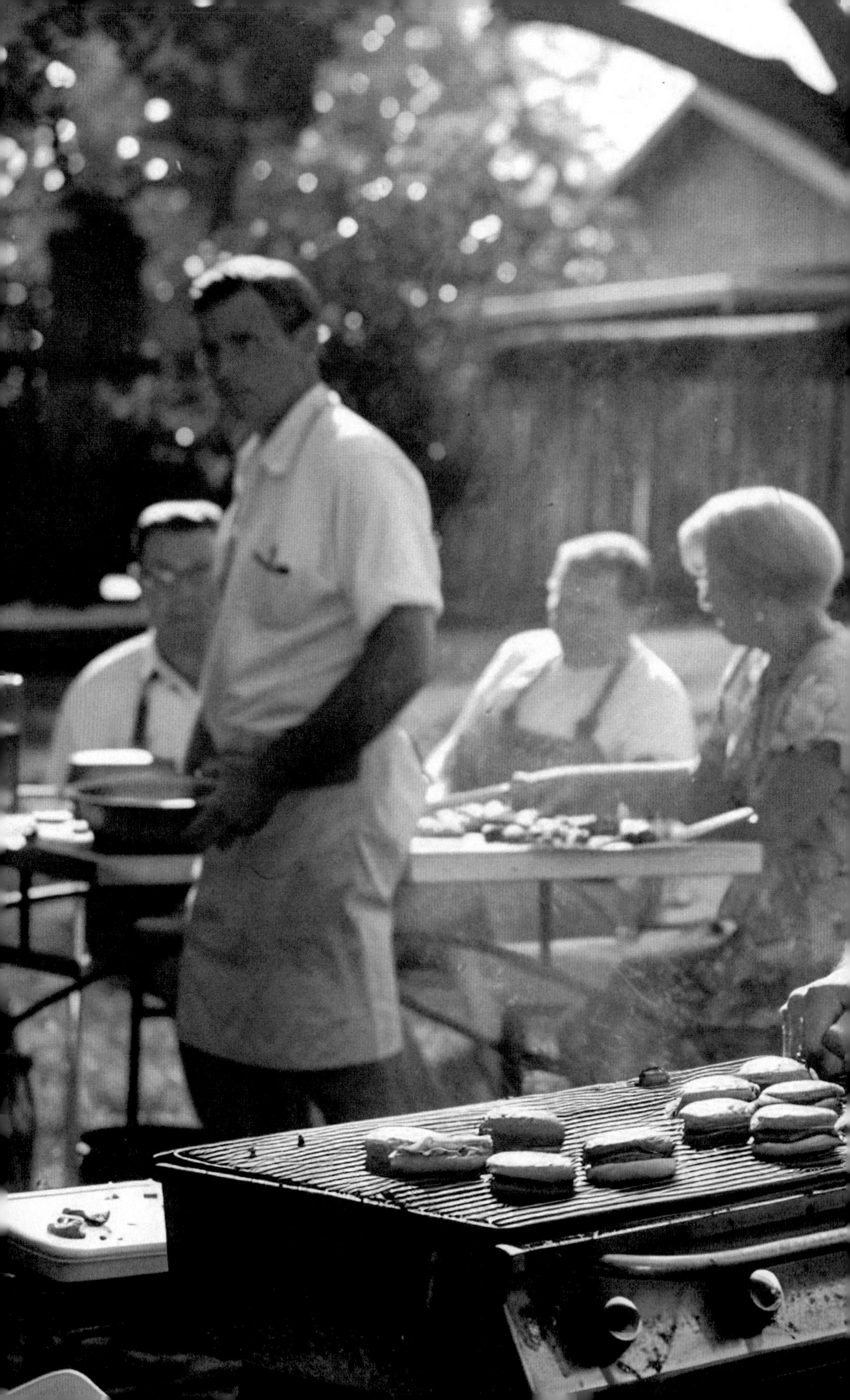

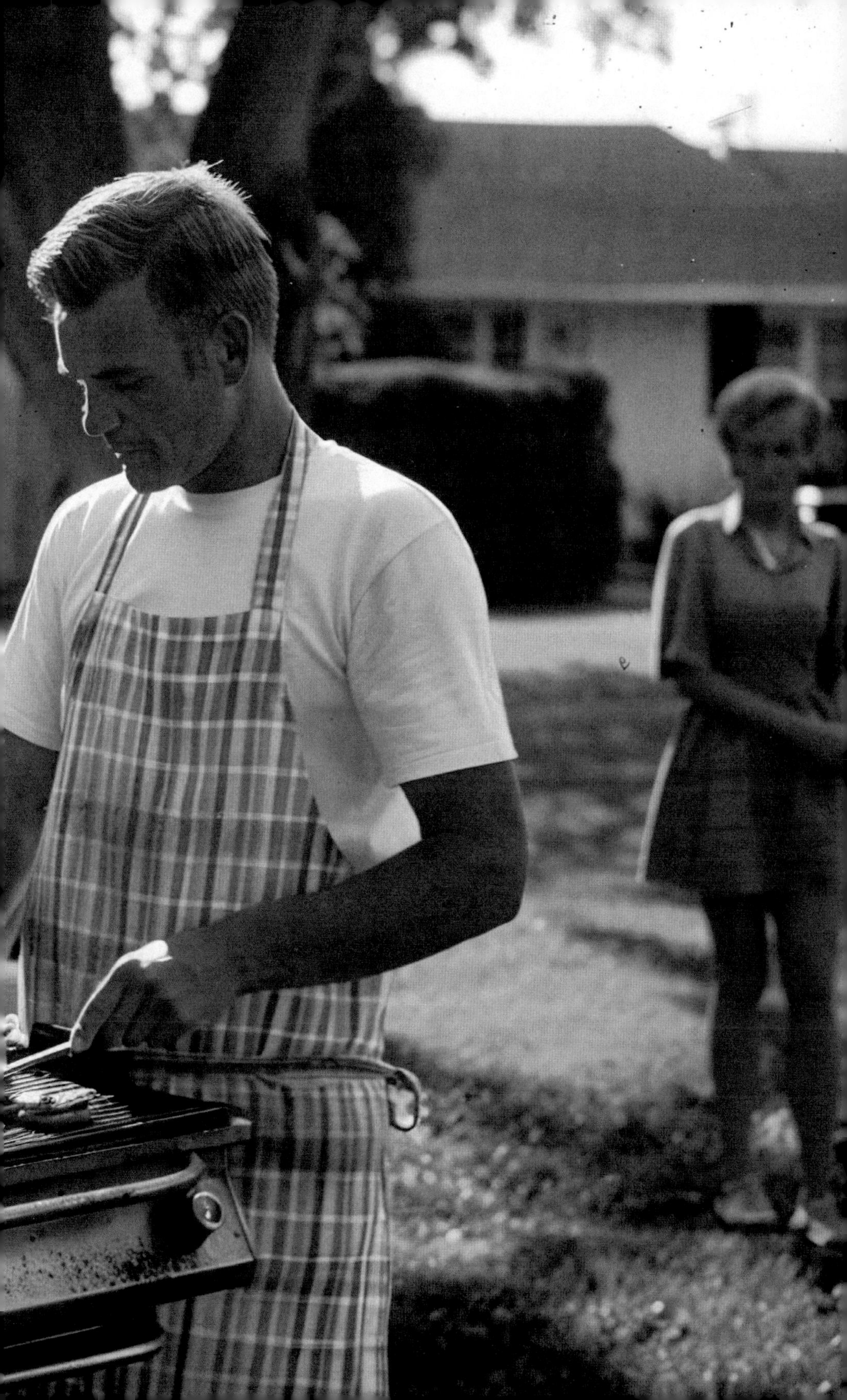

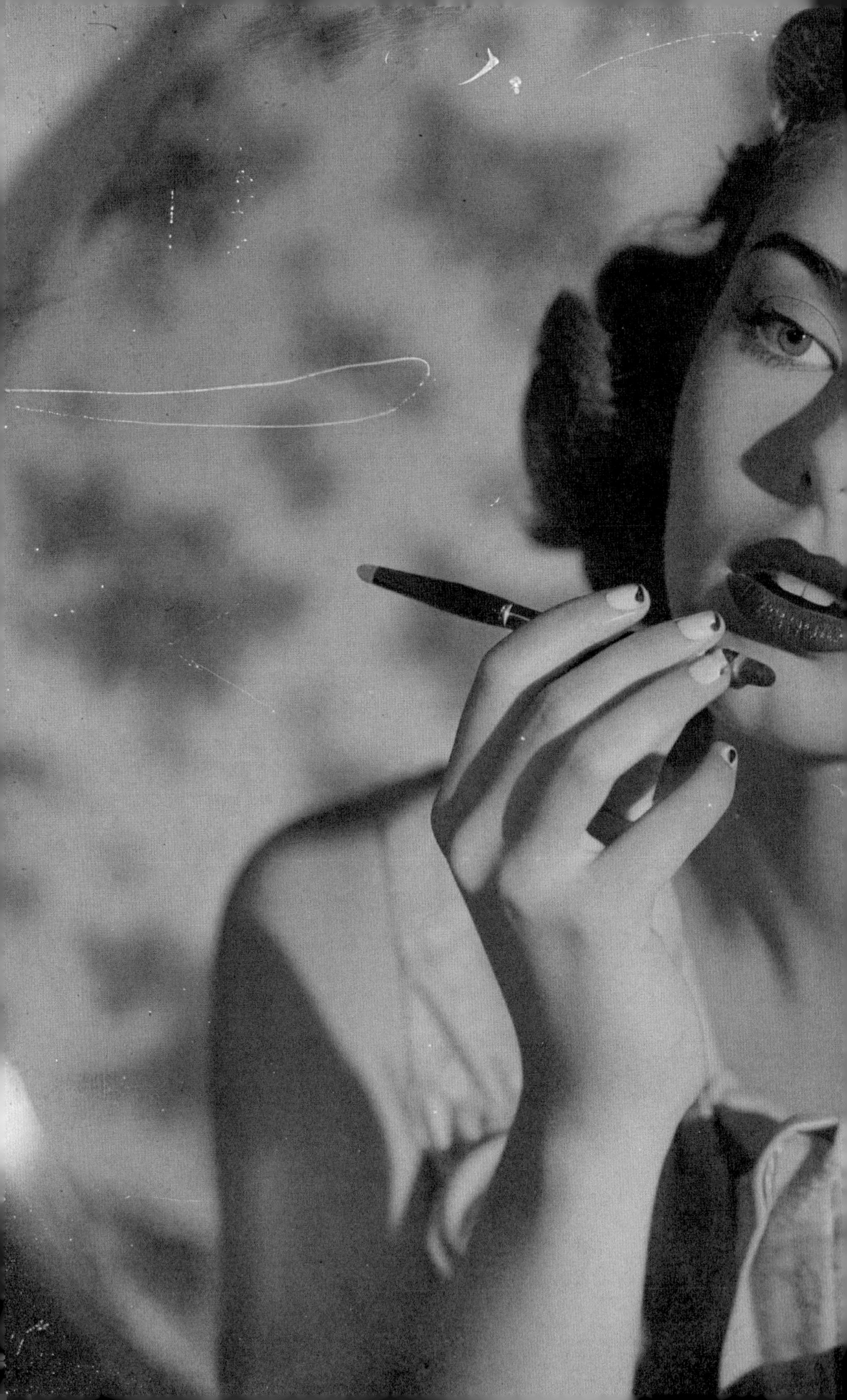

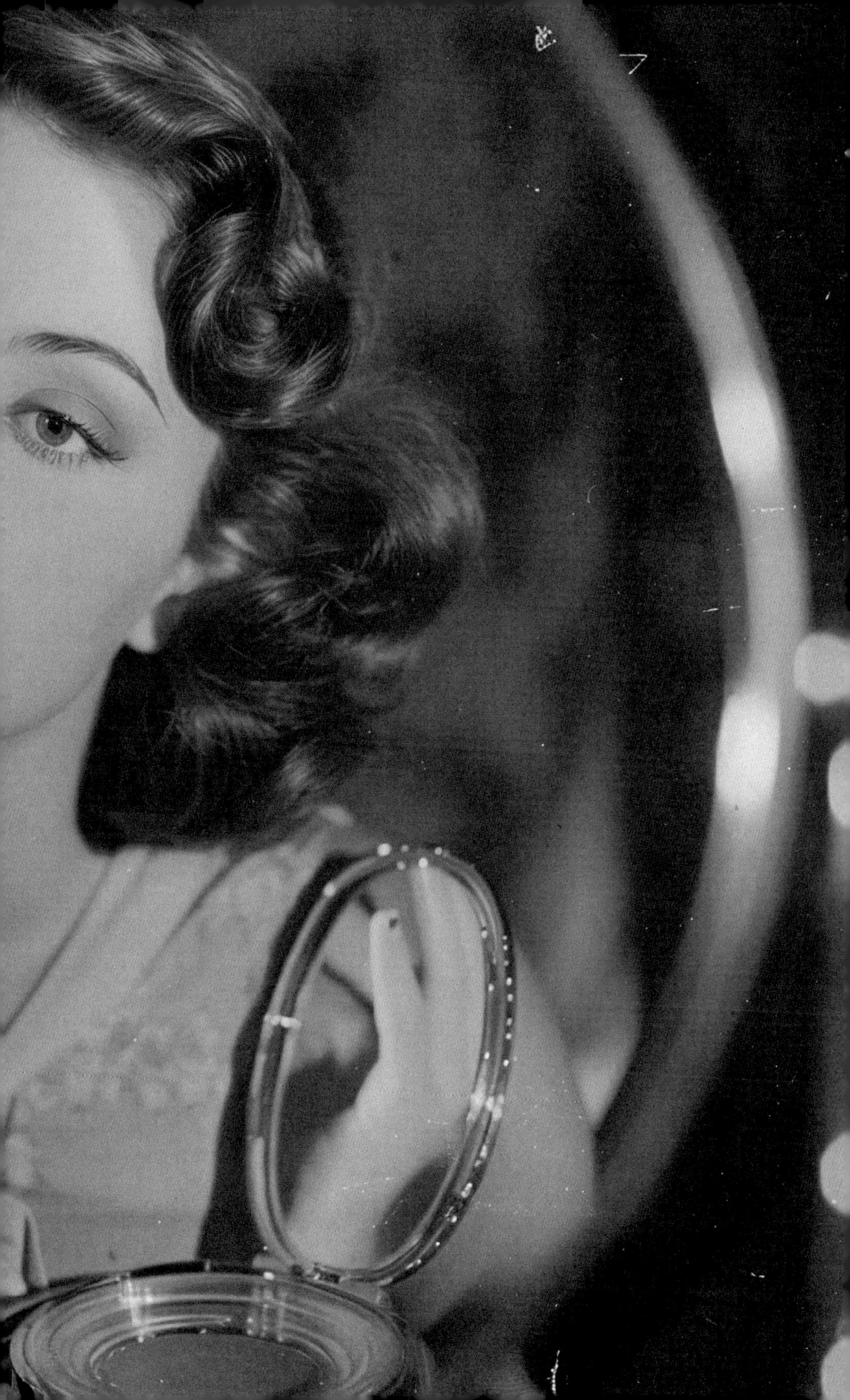

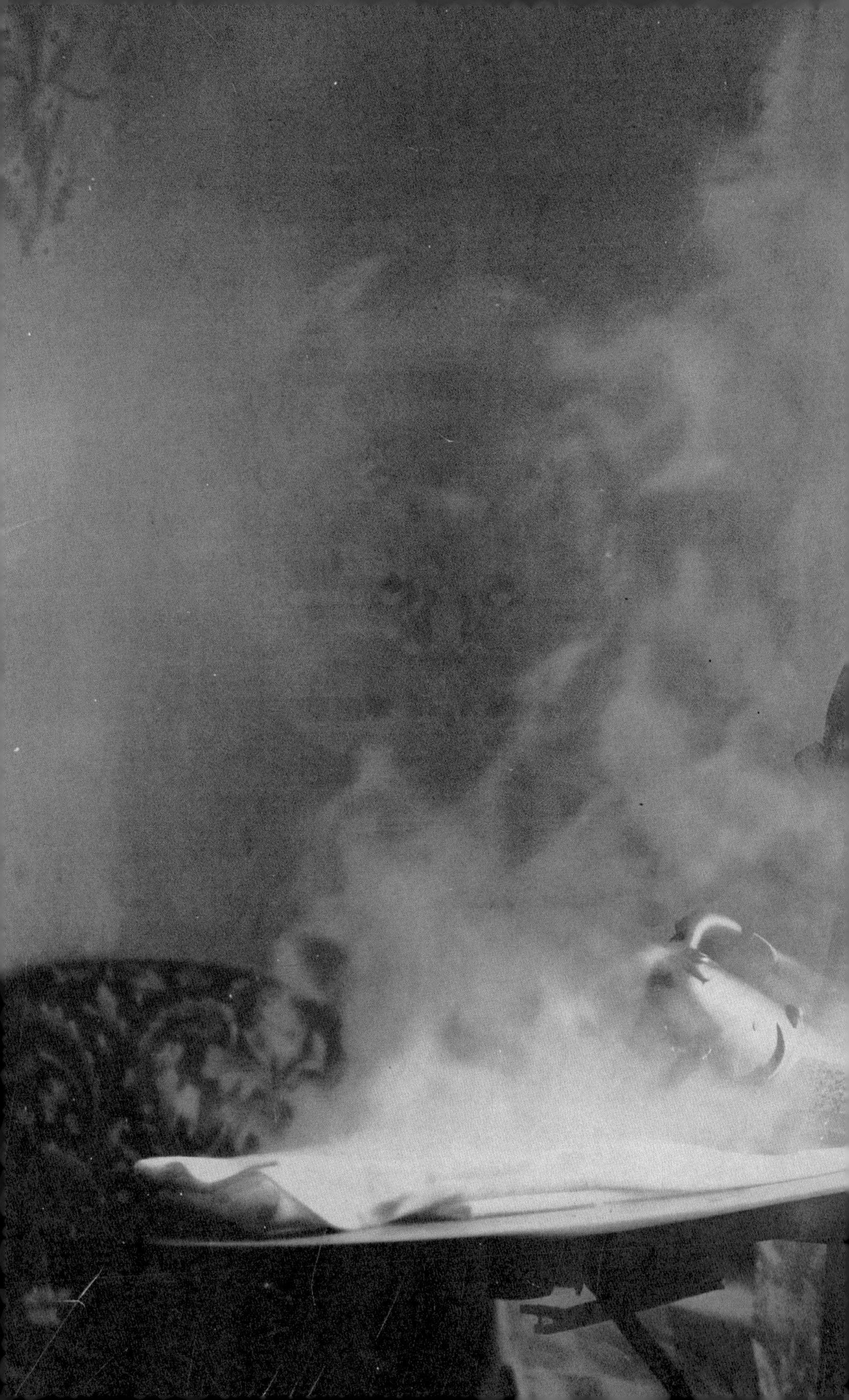

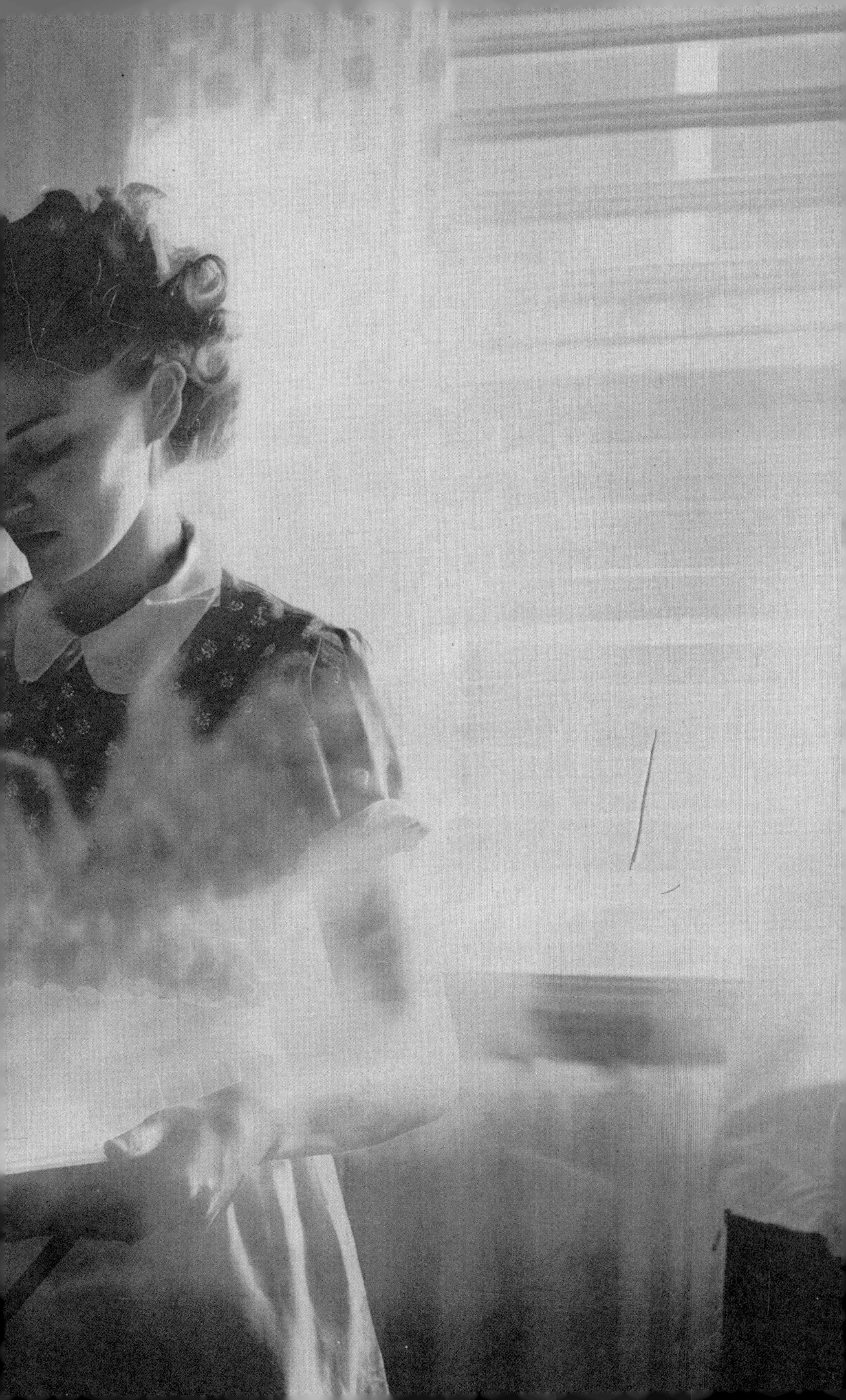

Made in the USA
Las Vegas, NV
09 December 2024

13665037R00026